PASSAGES OF A PASTOR

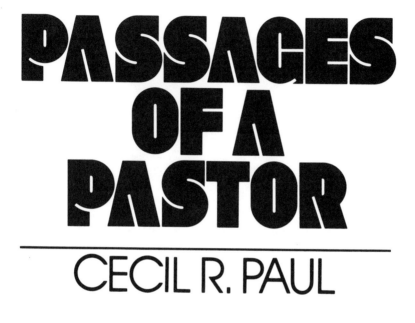

PASSAGES OF A PASTOR

CECIL R. PAUL

ZONDERVAN
PUBLISHING HOUSE
OF THE ZONDERVAN CORPORATION
GRAND RAPIDS, MICHIGAN 49506

PASSAGES OF A PASTOR
Copyright © 1981
by The Zondervan Corporation
Grand Rapids, Michigan

Second printing October 1981

Library of Congress Cataloging in Publication Data

Paul, Cecil Rowland, 1935-
    Passages of a pastor.
    1. Clergy. I. Viening, Edward. II. Title.
BV660.2.P29   248.8′92   80-26195
ISBN 0-310-43070-4

Edited and designed by Edward Viening

Printed in the United States of America

*Dedicated with love to my wife Judy
and to our sons
Bruce, Wesley, and Jonathan.
Also dedicated to the many pastors
who have contributed to my
pilgrimage of faith.*

Contents

Acknowledgments

This book is an expression of my love and respect for the ministers I have been privileged to know. While the book contains composite cases to protect the identities of pastors, they do reflect the insights and concerns that have arisen from the many dimensions of my relationships with pastors. Any resemblance to a specific pastor is coincidental and due to the reality that there are common needs, tasks, and crises confronting the clergy in their personal and professional life experiences. The motivation to write this book has arisen from the depths of the counseling, consultation, and communication I have experienced with these men of vision, love, and commitment. It is my hope that this book will in some way make their burden lighter and contribute to the effectiveness of their ministry to others.

Dan Gresham has provided important consultation on form and style, and has contributed significantly to my motivation to work at the task of writing. Judy Abugelis typed, proofread, and enthusiastically encouraged the development of the manuscript.

1

The Commission and Cry From the Heart

COMMITMENT UNDER STRESS

At a recent conference a pastor made a statement that reflects the impact of stress on the ministry. "I am seeing the results of stress on my life. I am beginning to wonder if it is worth it to stay in the ministry. I guess it is just getting harder to handle the stress of commitment. I can identify with Jeremiah 8:18 and 9:2." The first verse reads: "When I would comfort myself against sorrow, my heart is faint in me."[1] This statement is an identification of the limits of self-healing or self-care, and this is so often the feeling of the one who seeks to minister to the needs of others. The second verse reads: "Oh that I had in the wilderness a lodging place of wayfaring men; that I might leave my people, and go from them."[2] This statement is a somewhat angry or hurtful exclamation of a fantasy of escape from the stress of ministry. Whether to escape for a day or two or to flee the ministry altogether becomes the issue for the hurting helper.

Against this crush of reality the pastor remembers that commission that serves to stir his sense of being and becoming.

The Spirit of the Lord is upon me; he has appointed me to preach Good News to the poor; he has sent me to heal the brokenhearted and to announce that captives shall be released and the blind shall see, that the downtrodden

shall be freed from their oppressors, and that God is ready
to give blessings to all who come to him.[3]

It is in pursuit of the fulfillment of this call shared with Jesus
that many pastors enter the arena of human suffering. The
relative fulfillment of that call maintains the pastor's level of
motivation in the face of the pressures and stress factors inevitably involved in confrontation with the powers of darkness. Yet for many clergy today the balance shifts and the
sense of call is overwhelmed by multiple stress factors. Sometimes those stress factors are externally imposed, coming from
the demands of life and the expectations of the institutional
church. At other times those stress factors come from within,
representing the tasks and crises of the successive stages of
psychosocial development.

It is within this same Luke 4:18–19 that we discover
Jesus' sensitivity to stress factors. This passage takes us from
an idealized image of the ministry to the real world of challenge and critique. Jesus asks a central question when He
quotes the proverb: "'Physician, heal yourself'—meaning,
'Why don't you do miracles here in your home town like those
you did in Capernaum?' But I solemnly declare to you that no
prophet is accepted in his own home town!'"[4] Intimidation
from those to whom one seeks to minister is a clear reality in
the life of Jesus. It finally led Him to the cross. The very nature
of man's predicament of sin and sickness makes the healer or
helper a threat. It raises the polarities of hope and despair,
anticipation and disappointment, and expectations followed
by critique.

The challenge to the helper is as it was to Jesus the
Healer—heal yourself! The pastor is expected to have his life
together and to be untouched by the human element in his
personal life. On the other hand, the media has created a picture of the clergy as weak, lacking in normal human sensitivity, and out of touch with the realities of man's sin and sickness. He is caught in the middle of unrealistic expectations and
distorted stereotypes. The challenge does not end here. It runs
deeper and touches the integrity of his ministry. After all,

what is he really accomplishing? We have heard tell of miracles in Capernaum, so what is he accomplishing where he is? Joe Smith is doing great things in First Church while little is happening under his leadership.

It is normal to become defensive when pressured, stereotyped, and criticized. Even Jesus sought to defend Himself when He pointed out that the great prophets in their days also were not entirely successful. This merely served to infuriate that crowd who in their anger sought to throw Him over a cliff just outside the city of Nazareth. We today have hurting pastors who need to keep this passage in mind when they find members of their own fellowship seeking their termination. Jesus was so overwhelmed by the pain and hurt of seeking a ministry that He passed through the crowd and disappeared from their sight.[5] This runs parallel to the words of the pastor Jeremiah: "Oh that I had in the wilderness a lodging place of wayfaring men; that I might leave my people, and go from them."[6] The apostle Paul struggled with continuing opposition and barriers to the healing ministry, to the extent that at one point he shook the dust from his sandals and left a community to rot in its sin.[7] And we have pastors today who have struggled with both the rejection of the secular community and the opposition or passive resistance of the church itself.

ON BEING HUMAN

An obvious tension exists between the idealized fulfillment of the commission and the realities of ministering to man in his complex state of sin, sickness, and resistance. Therefore a major source of stress in the minister is the neglect of his own human limitations, needs, and life tasks. The minister faces the stress of physical overextension and the intense emotional investment of caring for others, and because of this the incidence of physical burn-outs in the middle years of the ministry is not that uncommon. The incidence of heart disorders also is high for the clergy.[8] The intangible nature of much work of the ministry invites the pastor to overextend himself, physically and emotionally, while trying to validate his ministry to his congregation and to himself. The very process of caring for others puts the pastor in touch with needs, tasks, and discrepancies in his own private life. This continued self-consciousness brings to the minister a whole new inner-directed dimension of stress.

As the people filled the pews and the music filled the sanctuary, pastor Phillip Carlton found himself in a deep mood of reflection and introspection. Somehow the approaching service seemed terribly disconnected from the real world of pain and uncertainty he saw represented there that morning. It was as though people were wearing masks that served to hide their anguish and confusion. The polite and precise behavior of Jim and Helen represented the competence they had demonstrated in raising two fine children to their college years. This couple in their late forties appeared to others in the church as models of stability. Actively involved in the life of the church, they were often invited into leadership and fellowship. That morning he saw them in a new light, for they had just that week unloaded their hidden problems. Much to Phillip's surprise, a routine pastoral call led to their informing him of a great emotional gulf between them that had caused a complete breakdown in communication. They felt the impact of losing their children, around whom so much of their relationship had developed. Helen spoke honestly of her feeling of deprivation and loss in both her early childhood experience and in her years of marriage and family life. As she sought new directions and meaning for her life, she saw Jim as pulling away from her. He perceived her as meeting all his needs. He knew her as an effective mother, so what could be wrong with their marriage? A psychological divorce was taking place and neither knew how to recapture commitment and communication.

The pastor's reflections on their situation shifted to introspection as he noticed his own wife, Sarah, in the congregation. Phillip and Sarah had raised their three children to independence and Sarah was going through a period of self-evaluation and decision-making. Phillip had found her to be quite depressed and nonresponsive in recent months. In somewhat the same pattern as Jim, Phillip found himself feeling isolated, frustrated, and confused. He was beginning to feel a failure in his own marriage. What did this do to his sense of integrity in ministering to others such as Jim and Helen?

Attempting to escape this process of introspection, the pastor looked to the back of the sanctuary. He had been counseling a fifteen-year-old boy who entered the sanctuary, hesitated, and then quickly slipped into the last pew. Mark was at church due to a combination of parental expectations and rapport with the pastor. The rigid religious demands of his parents were implemented in an authoritarian atmosphere. Mark had found in the pastor the acceptance and listening ear he needed. While this made the pastor feel good, he found a different focus for his thoughts that morning. His mind went back three years to the time when his oldest son, Steven, was a senior in high school. Due to his preoccupation and involvement in ministry, he had invested little time in building a strong relationship with his son. An altercation over Steven's decision to drop any college plans aggravated the hurt, anger, and lack of communication that had characterized their relationship at that time. While that experience had increased his sensitivities to the needs of the adolescent, he continued to struggle with guilt over those years in his ministry when he had neglected his own family's needs.

Seventy-year-old Sam Taylor, one of the true pillars of that congregation, sat in his usual pew that morning. He was a man who had consistently practiced Christian stewardship throughout his life, but that morning he was a picture of loneliness. His wife had passed away one month earlier, leaving him alone to cope with old age and his declining resources. Grief, complicated by some major economic pressures, made life for Sam an ongoing struggle. Whether to move two thousand miles to live with a son and family or to find a small apartment or room was not an easy decision to make. Phil saw his father in Sam Taylor that morning. He remembered how his father literally gave everything he had to minister to others.

As a retired pastor he found himself with no equity, a weak retirement program, and a loss of a professional role and its related purpose. Sarah's parents were also struggling with the tasks of old age. How were they to respond to these immediate family needs? Suddenly all his old sermons on responsibility to the elderly and lonely came crashing in on him that morning. The intense depth of involvement with people almost overwhelmed him. Whatsoever you have done in your church, do in your own home? Those people became a composite of his own personal needs, his private life. Feelings of commission, compassion, and confusion permeated his consciousness that Sunday morning.

REFLECTIONS

Wasn't he supposed to be at the peak of his professional life at the age of forty-three? He certainly didn't feel like it that morning. Everything seemed to be crowding him into a corner lately. What was blocking the realization of his dreams and aspirations that he brought to that parish five years ago? Was it time to change churches again? Would such a move place him in a new and untested situation that might prove even more disastrous? Was he losing his confidence? He found himself wondering if he had sacrificed his family's needs in pursuit of an intangible dream. He worried more about his own personal needs. Beneath the surface of his caring for others were concerns about his own age, health, finances, and directions for meeting needs, responsibilities, and expectations. He found it difficult to preach that morning, but as always he fulfilled his obligations to others.

The stress factors that impact the life of the pastor are multifaceted and complex in their interaction. The tensions between his sense of mission and the realities of the process of ministry are a significant part of that stress. The resistance and mixed expectations of the community and the church run counter to the fulfillment of his call. There are times when he is expected to be a spiritual superhero, untouched by feelings of personal infirmity and need. He is expected to have his head and life together. Yet, as stated previously, the media has created a picture of the clergy as weak, lacking in normal human sensitivity, out of touch with the realities of their parishioners' predicaments. The minister is often trapped between these contrasting expectations and distorted stereotypes.

These forces are in part responsible for his pattern of overextension, which serves to tax him physically and emotionally. Dedication to God and the call becomes mixed with motivation to validate his ministry to others, to meet their mixed expectations. He has become the representative of his congregation to the extent that he is their ministry as well as their minister. Thus they burden him with not only their needs, but also with their general expectations of the ministry of the church. All too often they abdicate their own discipleship and critically analyze his failure to fulfill what should be the expression of their own gifts. Many pastors report feeling overwhelmed by these pressures to the point that their own priorities in ministry become shaken.

The rapidly changing culture and the shaping power of the media and technology bring additional stress to bear on the role expectancies of the clergy. The institutional church feels this impact and is often influenced to adopt and utilize secular models, methods, and means of program development and growth. The pastor is often expected to lead and facilitate that process of change. The demands for diversification of role and function add new stress to the process of ministering to people in today's society. The pastor finds himself under pressures to update his professional strengths in wide areas of responsibility in church leadership. For many pastors this becomes a distraction from their earlier established priorities and preparations for the ministry.

As we have noted, the pastor experiences two types of stress in the process of caring for others. The first type of stress is the chronic overextension pattern leading to physical wear and tear and emotional exhaustion. The second type of stress involves the neglect of needs, tasks, and crises appropriate to his particular age or stage of life. The very process of caring for others carries with it the potential for increased self-awareness. His own personal needs and hurts often surface as he responds to the needs of others. The challenge to heal himself carries with it the power of guilt and anxiety which serves to undermine the pastor's confidence in himself. His own humanness confronts him. It is in confronting brokenness that he gets in touch with his own. As he explores the psychosocial and spiritual struggles of others, he may confront the struggle of his own soul. Becoming highly vulnerable at this point, the pastor may escape it by overextension or withdrawal. On the other hand, such confrontations with his own needs hold potential for personal growth and the renewal of his ministry. It puts him in touch with the realities of man's pilgrimage and pain. It brings him to a point of dependence on the source of all healing, placing him in a position to be ministered to. Yet that question raised by Paul Tillich rings in one's ears: Who heals the helper?[9]

2

Young Men in Ministry: Visionaries and Realities

And it shall come to pass in the last days, saith God, I will pour out of my Spirit upon all flesh: and your sons and your daughters shall prophesy, and your young men shall see visions (Acts 2:17).

THE VISION TESTED

"Where there is no vision, the people perish. . . ."[1] The young pastor experiences a keen sense of the relevance of his vision to the realities of our walk in darkness. Visions, if they are to be validated, need to be tested by reality. The processes of preparation are behind him and with high expectations he enters life's valleys where men perish without visions.

The prophet Amos proclaimed, "Behold, the days come, saith the Lord GOD, that I will send a famine in the land, not a famine of bread, nor a thirst for water, but of hearing of the words of the LORD."[2] While there is little question that we need a vision, we nevertheless function in resistance to it when it comes. It is into this world of tension, between the need for a vision and resistance to it, that the visionary journeys. At no point in his life of ministry will the "man of God" experience quite the same combination of vision, zeal, and energy. And at no time will he face such a high degree of discrepancy between his idealized image of ministry and the realities of our resistance. He will also encounter himself in ways he had not anticipated, as his own needs and personal tasks demand new responses of commitment.

John presented himself to the Springdale church following his seminary training. Both he and his wife, Susan, brought high expectations in their vision of ministry to that community. This town of twenty thousand had several large congregations that claimed most of the church-going members of that town. His church was one of a number of small, struggling congregations claiming some special vision for those who would perish. John's church had ninety-five on the rolls and on a good Sunday seventy-five in attendance. During his three years of ministry, he cleaned out the "dead wood" from the rolls, but this appeared to some members and to denominational leaders as a loss of impact on that community. He had brought into the church four new families with whom he had a strong sense of rapport. They had both captured his vision and continued to confirm its power to him. However, the church was having trouble assimilating the newcomers into the fellowship and ministry. John was troubling the stale waters of traditional roles and functions. The oldtimers had the patience to survive the brief ministries of other men of vision, and they were optimistic on one theme: they would outlive John's ministry.

Susan had come to the church with a vision of what her own role would be in "their ministry." She soon discovered that her role expectancy and that of the people did not coincide. They seemed to be conveying double messages: "Be a good model of everything but don't meddle with what has been." Susan had taken on the music program of the church and was making some changes and adding new music. Women who had been actively engaged in the program became resistant and critical of her leadership. Some of this was indirectly expressed and was coming back to the pastor. John was beginning to wonder if they hadn't erred in this particular area, and so differences surfaced with Susan over "his ministry" and her role in the life of the church.

The tension between Susan and John increased as each

felt increasingly frustrated with the people of the parish. It was mounting to the point where their marriage was affected. They were confronting the normal tasks of the young adult years, which served to compound the communication problems. Susan was pregnant with their second child and felt overwhelmed by family demands. A related issue was John's workaholic pattern and his unavailability to the family at a time when Susan felt most needed, yet most unsure of herself. Her visions of ministry, marriage, and family did not coincide with the realities impinging on her. These were difficult days for both John and Susan, and after three years of testing the vision, John was unsure of his ministry and troubled in his personal life.

The Scriptures reveal that God's servants will encounter powers that will test their vision. Paul, in writing to the Ephesians, speaks of principalities and powers of the realm of darkness (Eph. 6:12). As we compare the testings of Paul with the ministry today, we find little correlation. In fact, we experience testings in areas from which we would least expect opposition. Instead of outright persecution and opposition of the secular world (as Jesus and the early disciples experienced), we confront apathy and indifference. It is as though we would choose to perish before examining the vision. A society that either ignores or stereotypes creates high levels of stress for the visionary seeking dramatic change in the life of the community. There is a high casualty list of those who either lose their vision or leave the ministry.

The apathy and resistance of the secular order is not as stressful as the apathy and indifference of the church itself. The young man who brings his vision into the "community of faith" is often shocked to find little faith and limited enthusiasm over ministry to others. Beyond the apathy he experiences in the parish he may, in fact, encounter resistance for the ways in which he seeks to make that vision operational. The parish, too, would rather die than change. John found himself under criticism for his outreach ministries on the basis that they upset the pattern of worship, fellowship, and education in the church. He found himself drifting away from his vision toward a significant degree of cynicism.

There are two areas crucial to our understanding of the nature of stress and stress management in ministry. The first of these involves the psychosocial history of the pastor. What unresolved crises and tasks continue to influence his perceptions, expectations, and responses in ministry? The second relates to the normal and current tasks appropriate to the young adult stage of living. Perhaps we have too long neglected the human vessel through which God makes His message known. The young pastor may come into the ministry without an awareness of his own psychosocial history and its continuing impact upon his needs and responses. He may be unaware of the degree to which these figure into his reception and understanding of the call to ministry. He may also enter the ministry unprepared for the common tasks and needs of the young adult years, and the degree to which these connect with the quality of his ministry. If a man is not freed from bondage to unresolved crises out of the past and unfulfilled needs in the present, his ministry as well as his own health and growth may be jeopardized.

FOUNDATIONAL GROWTH EXPERIENCES

Few vocations demand such a powerful expression of the sense of identity, values, attitudes, and competencies as the ministry. The sense of vision is directly related to both the positive and negative psychosocial forces operating in the minister's life. How he defines man's needs and God's responses may be more dramatically connected with his own pilgrimage than with his educational experience. The refining of his theology, whether systematic or practical, and the development of skills may in fact be guided by his own choices and filtered through his own psychosocial history, which was also a spiritual pilgrimage.

Erikson has identified the young adult years as those involving the psychosocial crises of intimacy versus isolation. The task is to effectively enter into meaningful dimensions of intimacy and reciprocity or to shrink back and withdraw into a posture of isolation.[3] The quality of balance or degree of polarization between intimacy and isolation was set in motion during one's earlier developmental experiences. To the young adult the unresolved crises of past history may serve to block the quality of current intimacies and task fulfillment. The young person in ministry is no less subject to these forces. Insight into these forces may enrich his ministry with qualities of self-awareness and help him achieve authenticity of communication. Getting in touch with his own psychosocial experiences may facilitate his understanding of the people to whom he ministers.

Those qualities that are crucial to our response to the crisis of intimacy have been identified as trust, autonomy, initiative, industry, and identity. These facilitating forces enrich the quality of intimacies in the young adult years. Other forces serve to block and inhibit the socialization process and drive us into isolation. These barriers are the carriers of past experiences built on mistrust, shame, doubt, guilt, inferiority feelings, and a confusion of identity.[4] No other vocation deals more directly with such forces, whether expressed as sin or sickness, than does the ministry. If those forces operate in the pastor's own life, and beneath the threshold of his own awareness, how can he effectively enter into the crises in the lives of others? Both pastor and people will perish without an enlightened vision.

Figure 1 illustrates the dynamic and evolving nature of the individual's psychosocial history.[5] The early childhood crises orbit the new emerging core of intimacy versus isolation. The crises pull on that core, determining its characteristics and influencing its directions. If the forces of trust, autonomy, initiative, industry, and identity are most powerful, the quality of intimacy and its direction will be positively influenced. If those units of experience are primarily mistrust, shame, doubt, guilt, inferiority, and identity confusion, the movement will be toward isolation. These cells of human experience continue to operate in our lives and filter into our ongoing development.

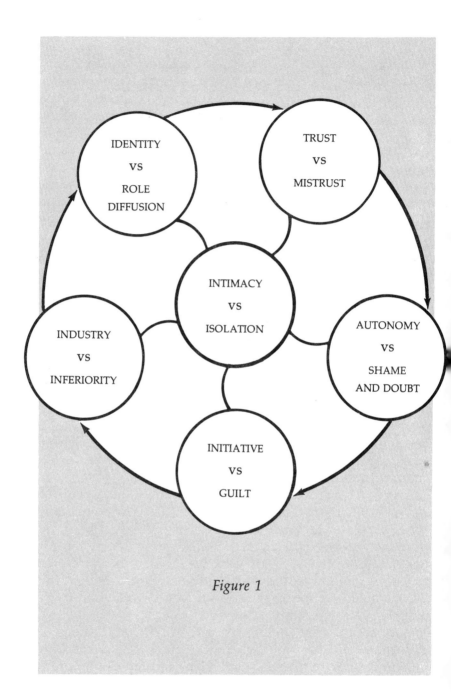

Figure 1

Those early experiences with the crisis of trust versus mistrust are primary to a person's approach to the demand for intimacy. Trust becomes essential to the reception of a vision and a call. When the message of the messenger is built on early mistrust experience, it is more reflective of the individual's own deficiencies and fears than of a positive sense of the availability of love and grace. When the source of the vision is the individual's unresolved crisis of mistrust, it is likely that the communication will be loaded with elements of judgment, criticism, and coldness. Then the message fails to bring hope of reconciliation to those who perish. The critical demand for authentic, intimate community is met with mistrust and the related feelings and actions of anger, fear, and isolation.

Elements of mistrust are inevitable and to some degree essential to survival. The individual who has been overprotected and overindulged is likely to develop a credulous and self-centered posture toward life and people. This person is ill-equipped to cope with the crises and demands of successive stages of development and is unprepared for the disappointments he will experience in working with people. He may be hurt in areas of intimate communication due to the vulnerability of naive optimism. The humanistic philosophy of life, which influences the thinking of some clergy, comes out of a strong wish and will for goodness to reign on the human scene. This vision may be so based on belief in self and human resources that the need for God and His work of reconciliation is lost. For the young man in the ministry, such an optimism and hope in people confronts the darkness and resistance of people and their institutions. This has led some pastors into disillusionment and an isolation from the ministry. In some cases, the trust in their philosophy is maintained and their cynicism is directed at the institutions that they perceive as resistant. It is the society and the environment that have violated the vision rather than those who have chosen to resist the vision and perish in their own sin.

It is important to depart from the continuity and determinism of Erikson's system to note that dramatic changes do take place in the lives of individuals who have known significant crises of mistrust. Many clergy have come through the negative polarities of psychosocial experience and have through combinations of peak mystical spiritual experiences and a dependable and loving community become as new creatures. Their vision for the people who perish is fueled by their own experience in perishing without the vision. They grow in their own ministry and authentically relate to the community of believers. They, with their people, grow up in the body and mature in faith and life. And yet it was through faith built on trust that such dramatic life change took place.

Elements of mistrust continue to operate in most of our lives, and many struggle with them all their lives. They function with the commitment of "I believe; help thou mine unbelief."[6] The commitment is not based on feelings, for if it were it would be lost. These elements of mistrust continue to operate within the church community. The pastor who carries deep scars of mistrust may have periods of depression and significant stress. He is expected to be the facilitator of an intimate caring community. At times he shrinks back from such intimacy into isolation and mistrust, particularly if current stress factors such as resistance and rejection within the community reinforce his earlier experiences of mistrust.

A vision built on trust, both human and divine, is a vision that will withstand the pressures, demands, and resistances of the people. The individual must learn how to give and how to receive, how to allow flexibility and adaptability to operate in his communications. He maintains his vision that reciprocal love and trust are essential to man's survival. His confidence is that this love and trust is ours because God first loved us. When a pastor doesn't have this or loses this, the stress of ministry to others will increase beyond his level of endurance.

Autonomy in the developmental experience includes the positive traits of exploration and production. A person's later development depends on these foundational experiences for confidence and competency. The young adult confronts tasks that will test him out for these strengths. The minister, both personally and professionally, is continuously challenged at this point. When the polarities of shame and doubt are present to an unusual degree, the pastor may struggle with a lack of confidence and a doubt of his competency or even his message. He is easily intimidated and may shrink from productivity and lose his vision. The normal task demands of the young adult (which we explore in more detail in the next section) may overwhelm him and preoccupy him to the point of keeping him from a healthful exploration of the multiple facets of intimacy and its expression in ministry. He may pull back with a sense of shame or humiliation, a sense of naked deficiency. His doubt about himself functions to undercut his communication of the vision and his follow-up ministry. Doubt about oneself can be one of the most significant weaknesses in the minister's coping capacity.

On the other hand, extremes of autonomous experience and behavior lead to insensitive communication with and behavior toward people. Patterns of holding back from intimacy and/or attacking people may follow. This is the individual who may assume some right to control the lives of others. He runs roughshod over their territory and dignity, and creates the potential for humiliation, shame, and doubt in their lives. The pastor who functions out of this posture perceives the church and its program as his. He so holds on to authority that he cannot let go of roles and functions that need to be delegated to the laity. Authentic expressions of intimacy cannot be built under this type of leadership. While he may pay the price with loss of confidence, and in some churches the loss of a recall, he tends to project the blame and shame on the church. The tragedy of this figure is twofold. He never realizes his own potential and he leaves behind a trail of hurt congregations.

Initiative is defined as the capacity to productively intrude into the environment. The crisis of intimacy demands the delicate balance of constructive and reciprocal intrusion. Initiative involves the capacity to mutually love and respect one another; to give each person the psychological space to be and to become. Two or more people enter into the lives of others with a sensitivity to the needs and readiness of others. Both marital and church relationships carry this potential for positive initiative but also the potential for guilt. It takes a strong pastor to manage these forces in both his own life and those of the community he pastors. If the pastor is lacking initiative, his people will not reciprocate and this will in turn further the process of guilt in his life. But too much initiative may so overwhelm the people that they feel violated and usually angry. So the tendency is toward isolation and behavioral withdrawal. This is where Susan may have intimidated and threatened the people. She intruded into their territories, assuming they would be delighted with her skills. Instead she drove them into hostility and isolation from her.

The function of guilt in relationship to initiative is particularly important in the life of the pastor. He may carry unresolved guilt in his own life and may assume a posture of negative, critical intrusion into the lives of others. If he has unresolved sexual conflicts, he may assume a prophetic function of rather continuous critique of the sexual mores of society. Such a preoccupation and investment of time and energy certainly serves to detract from the more critical positive process of building healthful intimacy into the fellowship of the community he pastors. One may be so guilt-riddled and unresolved at this point that he may continue to seek self-control through an intrusive control of the sexual lives of others. His preoccupation with this area of human morality may shift the balance away from other moral and ethical issues having to do with justice and reciprocity in human relationships. When this guilt element so dominates his life, it serves to block the quality of reciprocal love and care within the community.

Unfortunately, the pastor who struggles with personal guilt over sexual and aggressive feelings may function in such isolation that he is without resource. He may not be hard on his people but neither will he be sufficiently resolved to function as the facilitator of an intimate and caring community. Charles had pastored three churches, leaving each parish with limited success and with feelings of guilt over failing to bring his vision into the lives of his people. His own life had been one of an ongoing battle with guilt. His spiritual life was as unpredictable as his fluctuating emotional pattern. He had trouble separating his emotional state from his spiritual victory or defeat. The tragedy is that too many pastors carry this painful struggle over a period of years without either a significant other or a support system to help them sort out and find resources for victory. A significant other is a confidant who respects one's personhood and shares the truth in a manner that facilitates self-actualization.

Our middle childhood years are not really left behind us. Those are the years of developing industry through cooperative endeavors with others. Industrious expressions of one's skills within the social structures are foundational to how one will respond to the crisis of intimacy and all the related tasks of the young adult years. There is Michael who, as a young man in the ministry, has had recurring problems with self-confidence and a tendency to isolate himself from close relationships and small group activities. This is consistent with his middle childhood experiences of feeling inadequate and inferior to his peers. In fact, it becomes apparent that for Michael the ministry represents ways in which he might gain recognition and status with his adult peers. However, he is poorly equipped for the demands of the ministry which only serve to reinforce his experience with failure and low self-worth. Shared leadership and the capacity to cooperatively produce are important skills that bud in our early years. Competencies are both internally felt and externally expressed. Arthur expresses a great deal of external competency but is torn up inside due to internal feelings of incompetency. Somehow he never quite measures up to his expectations or his perception of the expectations of others. No matter what the demands of any parish might be, he is already under stress due to these perceptions and expectations. He may perceive his parish as he does himself: weak, inadequate, and without possibilities. It becomes apparent that prior experiences with doubt and guilt compound the problem with inferiority. The prior question to the crisis of intimacy is that of identity. The commandment of Jesus to love our neighbor as ourselves is a powerful statement of the truth that we have to have a clear sense of acceptance (which for the Christian is by grace) before we are able to effectively love others. In a vocation that proclaims the message of love, the messenger's strength in communication is that he possesses a clear sense of identity and personhood. This is true in his personal, marital, and family life, and also in his becoming a facilitator of Christian community. The visionary without an identity may move through periods of alternating zeal and, as a "true believer," function dogmatically only to shift as a ship with an unstable rudder. When identity is not integrated and directed, the capacity to build meaningful deep intimacies involving fidelity and commitment is weakened. It may be evident in behavioral withdrawal. However, it may take the form of what appears to be intimate behavior, but which in reality is a superficial substitution for mature intimacy.

Pastor Simpson had a honeymoon of a first year in the parish experiencing much enthusiasm and activity in the church. A fine preacher, he attracted some new people. But during the second year of his ministry he began to have evident problems. His marriage was in trouble due to neglect and indifference. While he had drawn some new people into the church through his preaching, he was having trouble integrating them into the fellowship. The personal and professional demands of the ministry took for granted the capacity to function intimately. Both his marriage and the church community were on the edge of new possibilities, but his tendency toward emotional and behavioral isolation was sabotaging this potential. This was not a new theme in his life. Most of his successes both academically and musically were through the utilization of his talents and personal discipline. He had a history of few friends and limited peer group involvements. Now, however, he was at a stage in his development and involved in a career that demanded capacities he did not experience or develop.

Pastor Jones had a similar experience with the churches he pastored, seldom staying for longer periods than two to three years. Establishing a strong and intimate fellowship was something he could neither understand personally nor demonstrate skills for professionally. It appeared that he moved frequently to avoid being caught as deficient. His aspirations for success were unrealistic and served to compensate for his ongoing struggles with each successive congregation.

Pastor Williams also evidenced a similar pattern of isolation. He would gather a number of strong supporters and would form a close-knit ingroup. They would function in radical isolation from and critique of the surrounding social order. Mistrust and hostility toward outsiders became increasingly evident. His own history of feeling different from others now became his identity. He carried the conviction that he had the final word of truth, and one got the feeling that it was his word rather than "His Word." Those who dared to disagree with him were soon forced out of the fellowship. The superficial appearance of intimacy within the community was really what Erikson refers to as incestuous sameness.[7] The tragedy of his ministry exhibited his own historic tragedies which had never been resolved. His early experiences with mistrust, shame, doubt, guilt, and inferiority fueled his radical attempts at finding both an identity and a community.

The man of vision is also a man who knows reality. Perhaps the power of his message is dependent on his grasp of the realities of man's struggles and needs. As his master, Jesus, entered the arena of human suffering, so, too, he knows the pain and struggle of the journey. What is unfortunate is that many never grasp the impact of that struggle on their current tasks and needs. This lack of insight or lack of congruence undercuts the power that grants integrity to their communication and their ministry.

CURRENT NEEDS AND PERSONAL TASKS OF THE CLERGY

It is evident that the psychosocial process is a pilgrimage in the lives of the clergy. It is also important that we grasp what needs and tasks are currently operating in the pastor's young adult years. As he responds to the needs of others, he needs to become increasingly aware that the human element and life's demands continue to make an impact on him. The tasks of others are often his tasks, and their needs and crises are often mirror images of his own. It is in losing sight of this that the pastor undermines his coping and communicating capacities. Sometimes he functions within a community of people who need to have him on a pedestal of holy otherness. If he, too, needs this for some reasons of compensation, his vision may be so idealized and out of touch with reality that the people will perish in his presence. Sometimes he will function within a community of people who need to have him on a cross. They will not give him space to be human and yet continue to find his human flaws. This may drive him into a self-protective retreat from authenticity. He withdraws from an open style of communication due to the fear of rejection. Both the pastor and the people need to value the pastor's particular life and pilgrimage with all its normal and unique tasks and crises. What may appear to the minister to be a distraction from his vision, may in fact be the power that enables him to communicate care and compassion as did his incarnate Lord.

One might assume that the spiritual leader is adjusting well and is effectively dealing with all the personal needs and tasks that might arise in his life. And yet the tasks and crises are there and carry the potential to enrich his ministry.

One of the most commonly or universally cited tasks of the young adult years is that of operationalizing the intimacies we just explored. Havighurst sees this in terms of selecting a mate and consequently identifies this as a central task of the young adult years around which the other needs develop.[8] Levinson sees this as one of the four major tasks for the "novice phase" and identifies it as the process of forming love relationships, including the family life experience.[9]

This is a central personal task in the life of most clergy. How successful they are in this personal area can have highly significant influence on how they are perceived professionally.

Many pastors report significant stress around such issues as marital problems and family life problems. It is often perceived by them (whether true to their people or not) as a reflection on their ministry. So many of the functions of the ministry focus on the family. The rites and rituals of the church are often connected with family life. The values and concerns of the people arise out of family experience and needs. The increasing problems with marriage and family life in America maintain this as a front-burner issue in the life of the minister as a care agent and representative of values to society. Whether he has marital and family problems or not, this pressure leads to his tendency to have high expectations of members of his own family. Some wives of clergy, as well as their children, feel they are too far down the list of his priorities of time and energy investment. This in turn leads to feelings of guilt for many pastors.

The task of selecting a mate may appear as secondary to the celibate priest or the single minister. However, he continues to function as a pastor to marital and family life crises. His own personal evolving need for intimacy is a natural part of his ongoing psychosocial development. Having made choices for celibacy tends to force him into situational isolation and separates him from both the personal support and potential stress of marriage and family life experience. Currently there is much debate over, and interest in, the possibilities of changing the laws of the Roman Catholic church governing the call for celibacy within the priesthood. Still there are fewer social pressures on the celibate priest than there are on the single minister, for the latter is often viewed as a candidate for marriage and is under considerable community pressure toward marriage.

Michael and Jane Ainsworth graduated from college, married, and went on to seminary. They pooled their resources, hopes, and aspirations along with their six-thousand-dollar indebtedness. The seminary experience introduced new role shifts, as Jane supported them both and he invested himself in another period of preparation. Michael continued to function out of traditional roles and leaned heavily on her for domestic support. The combination of wifely demands and economic pressures was eating at Jane. She began to avoid church participation with the excuse of fatigue and illness. Her anger toward Michael was directed toward the church and the call she perceived as locking them into such a crisis. Michael's insensitivity to this only served to compound the problem. He began to question her faith and her commitments, and this was received as basic mistrust and insensitivity. Their marriage was soon in jeopardy. Making a marriage function intimately and healthfully is no easy task for a young man in the ministry. Then, as they left seminary for their first church, they decided to have a child. The child introduced a second major task for young adult life and arrived coincidentally with the third major task of entering a vocational field of endeavor. These three tasks crowded in on them at a time when each task would benefit from a priority position.

Michael's first church was initially viewed by them both as a new start for them, as a time to rediscover the initial strengths in their marriage. The intruders soon surfaced. The financial pressures would not go away. The baby changed their private routine and added new stress to their lives. The church parsonage took on the characteristics of a goldfish bowl. What had been anticipated as a new start was becoming a source of new stress. For some pastors and wives this is not the case and they find the parsonage both a means of privacy and a means of getting over one financial hurdle of the early adult years, but Michael and Jane brought some unresolved personal and marital conflicts into the ministry. Consequently, the normal stress factors of the ministry grew out of proportion to their readiness to cope with them.

The task of commencing any occupation is a demanding reality; for those called to minister it is as difficult, or more so, as for those laymen who initiate themselves into the job market. In *The Seasons of a Man's Life* this is identified as one of the major tasks of the "novice phase" of development.[10] Establishing oneself in the ministry both excites and threatens the young adult, for it is unpredictable whether his goals and aspirations will be realized. Due to the complex functions of the pastoral role, the young adult in the ministry is immediately faced with more responsibilities and greater pressures than neophytes. There is little opportunity for apprenticeship, unless the young pastor selects the position of an associate minister. Depending somewhat on the polity of the denomination, he may be the chairman of most committees and boards, and be placed in a position demanding significant administrative skills. Furthermore, some congregations will look to him for the coordination of everything from fundraising to the Christian education program of the church. He may have approached the ministry thinking that preaching and care ministries would comprise the majority of his work. Now he finds he is expected to be an administrator, coordinator, educator, and public relations expert. Therefore, it is no wonder that his vision is frequently lost in a maze of complexities, as the young minister faces task after task while undertaking personal identity crises and suffering the loss of much personal need fulfillment.

Many pastors go through testing periods in which their call to the ministry is reevaluated. Some begin to wonder whether they are fulfilling God's call or someone else's perception of that call. This reevaluation may lead them to an awareness that the roots of their "call" are to be found in the influence of a particular layman, parent, or pastor. The stress of confronting this, and all its implications for their ongoing participation in the ministry, is heavy. As they reach the age of the late twenties or early thirties, pastors often consider the need for further studies, whether to sharpen their skills for ministry or to open up other options. With whom do they share these concerns? There is a degree of humiliation in confronting the possibility that they made a bad vocational choice or are not suited for the ministry. This is a vocation considered so sacred that to question the call lends guilt to the process. Where has the vision gone? If one did not exist, then what type of personality or character operates within? What if they discover that they do indeed have a call and that their vision is out of harmony with what the church as an institution expects of them? While this is more likely to occur while the pastor is in his twenties and thirties, it is critical that we emphasize that such identity and call evaluations are ongoing, and that during later periods of development and change they are more likely to recur.

"Finding a congenial social group"[11] is one of the young adult tasks with which most people would not expect the clergy to have difficulty. The clergy seem to easily meet this level of need, and, in fact, are considered by many churches to be the facilitators of social group activities. However, their participation is so role-related that for many spontaneity and reciprocity are missing. It is possible to be lonely in the group you lead. Pastors report feelings of separation and isolation due to a lack of freedom to authentically enter into the group process. Yet other pastors find this most comfortable because it provides them with a role and control of what is to be expected. Still other pastors are able to function comfortably in small group settings and identify this as the most rewarding and personally fulfilling dimension of their work.

Erikson views this need for intimacy and affiliation as inclusive of friendships and partnerships whereby "young adults become sons of each other."[12] These friendships and partnerships are based on choice, rather than the "blood bonds of family."[13] The pastor has a unique functional involvement in building affiliations for the people in his parish. While most pastors and wives reap positive dividends through the process of building these affiliations, for many the process of making friends is not easy. Some congregations so idealize the clergy that friendship bonds are not feasible for the pastor. He may be criticized for favoritism if he builds friendships with a few in the parish. The short-term ministry (under four or five years) seems to foster isolation from the process of building deep friendships. The minister and his family may refrain from making intimate friends; they do not "become the sons of each other."

The church is often called the family of God, an analogy used by the apostle Paul, because the church does carry tremendous potential to enrich the lives of a society that has lost its sense of the extended family. Many pastors and wives have lost the closeness of family ties and deeply need a sense of that extended family. Whether it is due to the pattern of short-term parish ministries or differences in viewing roles, pastors and wives (sometimes one more than the other) feel this as a common problem. It is ironic that the facilitator of affiliations is himself deprived of the enrichments and benefits of the social contacts he helps create.

Some congregations make it easy for pastors to build friendships; and, in fact, fully expect his friendship and support throughout his ministry. But the new minister is often undermined by the pattern and posture of his predecessor. If strong dyads or cliques were a part of the prior pastorate, the successor will experience two concerns. Cliques may expect him to fill the same role as the former pastor, or they may reject him on the basis of their special relationship with the former pastor. The remainder of the congregation, those not a part of that closed social unit, may be supersensitive to any signals that the same exclusive pattern may recur. Some congregations find it easy to accept the pastor's wife as a unique individual, while others have rigid and unrealistic expectations of her. Pastors and wives who survive most effectively are not intimidated by what has been, but give themselves and the parish some time for reshaping. They are most successful if sufficiently confident and mature, able to balance friendships and pastoral care without violating pastoral functions or their personal social needs.

Recently, many writers of adult developmental psychology have focused on a specific young adult need—that of finding a mentor and building a mentor relationship.[14] The mentor is the person to whom the young adult turns for consultation and support in times of crisis and decision-making. The mentor is a model of sorts, but more of a confidant, a sounding board, a means of both ventilation and clarification.

Confronted with the trial of his vision and the demands of personal and professional tasks, the pastor generally needs a mentor. The barriers to the realization of such a mentoring relationship are numerous:

1) He may feel vulnerable to the process of introspection and ventilation in the presence of another, questioning whether or not the mentor will respect him. As a result, he may hide his own sense of loss of self-respect and exude an over-idealized image of himself and/or his role, creating a barrier to the process.

2) He may feel guilt about needing such a relationship, seeing it as a negative reflection on his faith or dependence on God.

3) Following his college and seminary experience, he became isolated from the mentors he had established during those years. While he may continue to call on them in crisis, he may find that the time and space factors make this nearly impossible.

4) He may have trouble establishing such relationships within his own denomination due to feelings of vulnerability and even competition or political process.

5) On the other hand, he may not have developed relationships with clergy outside his own denomination and is not likely to seek out a mentor there.

Ideally, a senior pastor should function as mentor. A balance of vulnerability and ego strength may then be maintained by both. But judging from my experience, this is an uncommon occurrence. More often than not, some discomfort and confusion concerning other pastoral functions will surface. For example, Peter had a strong relationship with a seminary professor and was urged by that same mentor to seek out his senior associate. What followed was disappointing and served to undermine the surface rapport he had with the senior associate. Peter had long struggled with an incessant problem with authority figures, a difficulty easily traced to his authoritarian and demanding father. He had dealt with much of this by persisting in relationships with college and seminary faculty. The senior associate was not sensitive to Peter's past problem and assumed a paternal role that Peter found unacceptable. The senior pastor had to have the final say on most of the functions that Peter had been made to feel were his responsibility. While Peter was ready for a mentor, this high-risk relationship failed early and led to a staff separation. When Peter unloaded some of his cynicism and hurt, he found John cautioning him with fatherly wisdom. John also began to worry about Peter's loyalty to God and to the church and started holding back on what he considered to be the more delicate pastoral assignments. Within a few months, both of them knew that termination and change were inevitable.

The previously cited stress, a result of the dichotomy between the idealized image of the ministry and the realities one encounters, relates to one of the tasks Levinson and others identify as common to the young adult years. This is the task of "forming a dream and giving it a place in the life structure."[15] Young adult pastors are likely to respond to this need more intensely than most young adults. It has partially determined their identity since they realized their call and its related vision. During the years of forging an identity, it could well be that the values and purposes that evolved formed the basis for their dream and vision. Some discovered their dream through a deep and powerful mystical experience that enabled them to form a dream. That which contemporary authors are citing as an important task of these years was long ago identified by a prophet who saw this dream as a vision of hope to a broken world.[16] The early church was really built on the dreams of young men and women who dared to confront the stress of the world's resistance and to endure the cross and death triumphantly. The history of the Christian church is filled with dramatic stories of young men and women of vision who brought faith, hope, and love to a perishing social order. Young men in the ministry do bring those dreams and do continue to pay high prices for their commitments. Such visions trigger vitality in the church and reawaken in older ministers dreams long dead or dormant.

THE PASTOR AND COMMUNITY

Kenneth Keniston identifies the period between twenty and thirty as the period of youth for many young adults. For them, the central task is that of "negotiating a relationship between self and culture."[17] The task of adapting to the surrounding culture becomes a central issue in the lives of many young adults who see themselves as having something of a dream or vision to offer society. They often see themselves as facilitators of change and yet are confronted with pressures and demands to conform. The clergy are caught in the middle of such pressures. Perhaps there is no other profession in which this polarization is more likely to occur. The young adult who would aspire to the ministry is saying something about his care for people and the related issues of social evils and deficiencies. He possesses both a pastoral and prophetic sensitivity.

Many young clergy have not completed a negotiated relationship with culture. Jesus called His disciples "to be in the world yet not of the world."[18] There will always be a tension between caring and judging. However, such a posture is no less a negotiated and mature relationship than one of conformity. It is when the young adult goes through periods of alternation, from one position to another, that he signals a continuing problem with this task. As Keniston points out, he may shift from a radical position for changing society to a zealous commitment to separation through the carving out of a niche.[19] Another position they may assume, often around age thirty, is that of conformity.

The pastor has a twofold problem with community. He has the usual tension between self and culture, plus the issue of the relationship between his own identity and that of the institutional church. Many pastors are uncomfortable with the relationship between the denomination and/or local church and secular institutions and ethics. This is one of the most common sources of stress in the life of the young adult pastor. It is connected with the prophetic nature of his vision and thus is appropriate to his calling. The problem is that he is often locked into a posture of isolation from a "significant other" (mentor or priest) and support group.

The young adult in the ministry is often functioning on two tracks with respect to his identity and the culture. On the one track, he is attempting to determine how he wishes to relate to society and culture. On the other track, he is functioning as the prophet and leader of a religious community which necessarily assumes an evaluative posture in relationship to society and culture. Personally he may be struggling with the need to express his reactions against society. He may wish to reject its institutions and related values. His personal feelings and attitudes are of a radical nature. If he transfers this into his role as pastor, which one would fully expect him to do, he has now acquired a new problem. He may become actively involved in social causes with which his people may not identify. Others may, in fact, find themselves in polarization with him over such causes. Consequently, he finds himself relatively alienated or isolated from his own church as well as society. He may be functioning in a prophetic manner but naively assuming that his people either share his views or are ready to hear his positions relative to culture and the institutions of society (many of which involve his people in work and other social capacities). The stress on him and the congregation may be so great that the rapport and effectiveness of shared ministry is lost. His prophetic vision is just not shared by "his own people."

The pastor may wish to withdraw from society, urging his congregation to carve out their own niche and separate themselves from the world and its values. He may, in fact, begin to establish his own following and, as a radical pastor, might succeed if his followers are carefully shaped and then dissidents are forced out. If he succeeds in building such a separate community, he will likely begin to feel frustrated because his community is not growing and has little impact on society. As previously stated, one of the most difficult stresses to deal with is that of the apathy of others toward one's vision or message.

An alternative to the above separation is an attempt by the pastor and church to adapt to the surrounding culture and its values. However, the pastor who advocates complete adaptation, leaving no tension between the church's and the world's values and institutions, faces other stress. What is the point of it all? Does he have any vision to offer that is not more effectively presented by other care agencies or professionals? This question haunts many in the ministry who have assumed the posture of adaptation. Yet another source of stress is the reality that not everyone in the congregation feels the same way about society. Some are, as individuals, in constant conflict with the institutions and values that surround the church or are blindly accepting of even blatant social evils.

These tensions between self and culture and the church and society are ongoing realities in the life of the clergy. They peak during the young adult years in the ministry, years of vision, zeal, and vocational operationalizing. Again, how crucial it is that the young pastor find both a brother-priest or mentor and a strong support group.

Maturity in Ministry

Most personality theorists address themselves to the matter of maturity, focusing on those qualities or characteristics that enable a person to fulfill all the tasks of his young adult years, inclusive of the capacity to cope with related stress. As these characteristics are related to professional care persons, the focus is on effectiveness in working with people. What are the characteristics essential to the pastor's fulfillment of personal tasks and professional functions?

Carl Rogers and others emphasize the importance of self-acceptance in the mature adult.[20] This includes a combination of positive regard for oneself and an awareness of one's limits. The positive regard provides one with the confidence and motivation essential to taking the initiative in dealing with tasks and functions. This, combined with a sensitivity to one's limits, lends authenticity to communication. The individual who enters the ministry as a young adult with limited self-awareness will operate defensively and will thereby compound the stress of task and need fulfillment. The pastor assumes a role that is more likely to involve deep personal communications with people; therefore his self-acceptance becomes a critical factor in his effectiveness, an important part of his preparation. Most seminary programs and the clinical pastoral education requirements are directed to this need. It is my experience that the clinical pastoral training experiences are the most important in building professional readiness into the pastor. The most common point of positive reference is the stimulation to increased self-awareness and acceptance combined with insightful sensitivity to others.

Self-awareness and acceptance enable the young pastor to develop his capacity for openness to experience and other nondefensive attributes. Maturity for the young adult pastor means that he is open to change and is not rigid in his approach to functions and needs in others. Ambiguity is an ongoing reality in personal and professional development. The pastor who cannot deal with ambiguity is going to experience high-level stress. The task of building personal, marital, and professional intimacies into his life will be undercut if he lacks this quality of openness. If he approaches the ministry with a posture of rigid dogmatism and inflexibility, both he and his people will suffer. His vision will be phrased and presented in negative dogmatism which serves to polarize and antagonize. The prophetic posture is inevitably involved in the tensions between church and culture. Does the pastor always operate out of such a functional position? Can he effectively pastor and care for troubled people if he lacks open and nondefensive communication?

A related quality of maturity is the capacity to assume responsibility for one's own life and behavior. Rogers sees the functionally mature person as one who has an "internal locus of evaluation."[21] That is to say, his motivation and response to life are not based on external demands or dominated by outside pressures. Seen positively, the pastor is primarily accountable to God. The integrity of his ministry is his own experience of God's love and grace. He has internalized truth and grown in his understanding and skills to the point that he is not shaken by external pressures, demands, and evaluations. He is likely to be much more accepting and trusting of others and less inclined to project blame and responsibility onto either his people or denominational structures and leadership. Many young men in the ministry have a difficult struggle with the latter, a problem that frequently serves to undermine their ability to care for and communicate with their people without an element of cynicism surfacing.

Change is also an ever-recurring experience in life, particularly while attempting to help people struggling with their own developmental needs. The culture and its institutions are constantly undergoing change, and the institutional church cannot avoid this impact. The personality of the mature individual has developed the capacity to confront change and to effectively deal with it in his life, but a rigid and defensive personality has much difficulty with change. Combine the latter personal traits with a traditional approach to role and function and you have an immature person. The mature personality has the strength of self-acceptance combined with openness, so he is less threatened by change. He provides others with his resources of stability and flexibility, of openness and confidence.

A commonly cited quality of maturity is the possession of a *working philosophy of life*.[22] Certainly this is the clergy's strength. Christianity provides the minister with the essential framework for evaluating priorities and ordering his life. Thus the pastor is enabled to tolerate much stress in his personal and professional life due to the resources of his philosophy of life. It also enables him to minister to those who struggle with needs and crises that continually raise deep philosophical questions about life and values. Inasmuch as he enters the arena of human suffering, this becomes a most crucial quality for him to possess. Yet for pastors, intellectual doubts and struggles with the maintenance of their philosophy of life are commonly reported.

Having a faith to live by is another way of focusing this quality of maturity. His philosophy orders his life while his faith directs it, enabling him to live and love. The clergy, as a group, cope unusually well considering the evident and complex stresses that operate in their lives. I am convinced that it is a *faith to live by* that makes the difference. This is not to say that they, too, do not experience doubt and conflict. Actually, the testing of their faith is a common source of stress in ministers. Fatigue and overextension often bring clergy to the crisis of faith. Physical and motivational exhaustion, most likely to occur in later years in the ministry, do, however, occur in the young adult years. Inasmuch as their faith and the related spiritual and religious resources have been their primary shield and sword, there are bound to be some significant implications for coping with stress. Tragedy usually strikes when the young man of vision and commitment experiences the valley of despair with limited community, church, or spiritual resources. Without a vision he, too, will perish. That vision needs to be nurtured and fostered, for we so desperately need it.

3

The Ministry in Mid-life:
The Ins, Outs, and Ups of It All

Pastors in Crisis

Who would think that the clergy, well into the mature years of life, would experience anything but certainty of purpose and confidence in action? Who would anticipate that the thirties, forties, and fifties would be anything but years of stability coupled with the excitement of fulfilled vision? Certainly that young man of vision who entered the ministry ten years ago anticipated days of triumph and satisfaction. While he knew that some persecution was inevitable, inexperience lessened its impact on him. He had heard of ministers having personal problems and experiencing professional disappointments, but his life and ministry would be different. His vision would carry him through the testing he would face. He viewed hardship and persecution as externally induced, a reasonable result of the struggle with outside forces. The inward focus of spiritual experience and its outward expression in service to others would more than compensate for those testings. What he had not anticipated was the complexity of the fine distinctions he would be forced to make: i.e., the ins, outs, and ups of it all.

Mark arrived at the medical center with great trepidation. His wife's concern over his numerous physical complaints brought him to the doctor. On this, a day of confrontation with self, Mark was informed he was a prime candidate for a heart attack unless he slowed down, lost weight, and generally learned to handle stress. His recent complaints—chest pains, headaches, and exhaustion—were signals that he was approaching a physical collapse. Why was this happening to him? Hadn't he been spending his energies for his Lord and His church?

Mark is a real "driver" with little sense of his emotional and physical limits. He has pushed, pulled, and managed two churches through significant growth periods. Although these taxing achievements have critically affected his health, the problem runs much deeper. Others have paid a price for his success. He has either expected or allowed his wife, Carol, to carry the burden of managing his home and raising their three children. She has somehow insulated him from severe economic pressures by taking a part-time job unrelated to her earlier training or vision while in college. The continuation of her education has been postponed for thirteen years. However, six months ago Carol began to confront Mark with her needs and his history of neglect, which overwhelmed him and precipitated in his behavior contrasting patterns of withdrawal and episodic agitation. Beneath this erratic behavior lay a deep well of guilt. Transcending an unhealthy family situation—a remote, authoritarian father finally divorcing a doting mother —Mark began attending church in his teens and was converted at age sixteen. When he later married and started a family, he assumed his family life would be dramatically different from what he had experienced in childhood. But now his wife was confronting him with his own parental negligence, the consequence of which is immediate family strife. Having spent little time with his family, Mark now sees that what he had labeled "social life" was really an extension of his dutiful approach to ministry. Their oldest son, Robert, is having school and related peer group problems; so Carol confronts Mark with the fact that she was the one who visited the guidance counselor, while he was busy meeting the needs of "his people." The combination of his time and energy investment in his work, plus his anxiety and guilt over his mounting family problems, has become too much for him to manage. His body is signaling that the stress is overwhelming and something has to give.

Dwight has been pastor of the Parkdale church for six years, and during his ministry several families have left his parish. His limited efforts at outreach have yielded no evident results. During the last two years he has lost his incentive and finds himself marking time, and he is quite depressed. This forty-four-year-old man and his wife, Marilyn, have four children ranging in ages from fourteen to twenty-four. The oldest son, Peter, is a graduate student in political science. Their daughter, Sandra, is in college preparing for a career in teaching. Paul is a senior in high school, and John is in junior high. Raising their children well has been a high priority, particularly for Marilyn, who has never been career-oriented. The major domestic problem has been financial, intensified by the recent tuition expense. Dwight has had to work part-time and has never felt that his ministry was given the priority that he had envisioned.

Although he sees factors undermining his potential for significant achievement in the ministry, he wonders at times if he was misdirected in his earlier vision. During his early years he assumed that the preaching and teaching ministry would be his central functions. He has since discovered that the functions of administration and visitation do not excite him; in fact, he has found himself unmotivated in those areas. At times he has fantasized obtaining an associate to exercise those less desirable functions, freeing him to pursue his vision.

Dwight has explored his options. If he should stay in his present church, he risks further loss of motivation and with it his rapport with the people. On the other hand, he isn't sure he wishes to face the alternative of taking another church. He resists even the thought of reinvesting himself in the establishment of a new ministry in a new parish, with all the attendant uncertainties. Such thoughts make him both anxious and lethargic. Another option, leaving the full-time ministry and pursuing a different career, appeals to him in some ways.

Having excellent teaching skills, he would like to teach philosophy and/or religion at the college level. While this option excites him the most, powerful realities come crashing in on him. He should return to graduate school for a few years, but his children's educational and vocational needs currently have priority over his. "Perhaps I had my chance and failed!" he wonders, hurting as he considers this possibility. A final option open to Dwight is taking a six-month to one-year's leave from the pastoral ministry. Having secured a teaching certificate before attending seminary, he might possibly secure a one-year teaching position at the high school level. This would also provide opportunity for self-evaluation in a teaching environment, a situation he feels is of vital importance to him at this stage in his life.

Another pastor, Ron, fifty-two years old, has spent twenty-eight years in the ministry pastoring nine churches. During the six years in his present parish he and his wife, Eleanor, have completed the raising of their three children. Their older son, Alan, is married and quite indifferent to the church. Jean, who is married and raising two children, is actively involved in a church, but she and her family live in another state. Michael, the youngest child, is in college and is uncertain about the role of the church in his future. Ron and Eleanor have discovered that the primary basis upon which they had built their relationship was the children. The other foundation of their relationship was their shared history and experience in the ministry of the church.

During his first four years Ron experienced unusual success in outreach and growth, both numerically and financially. The past two years have not run so smoothly, however, although Ron's present church is the largest and strongest of his charges. Some of his lay people now express concern over his preaching ministry, the implication being that he has run dry and that they need a change. As he reviews the past two years he sees some personal problems as important to the picture. Eleanor, struggling with a chronic history of depression, dropped into a deeper level of depression three years ago. But neither of them has felt comfortable about letting the church people know of her difficulty. As a result, she endeavors to function within traditional roles but has not functioned well in her own home. During the past six months she has been seeing a psychologist and taking antidepressants under psychiatric supervision. Ron has reordered his priorities of time and energy investment, giving more of himself to her at this critical time in their lives. While responding to her crisis, he has found himself looking inward, and discovers deep feelings of personal loss and disappointment: disappointment that Alan is not in the church and a loss of hope in fulfilling his own vision for ministry. While experiencing good, solid success in most of the churches he has pastored, he had anticipated much more. He has never played a role in denominational leadership. Younger men are now holding higher office in the denomination. Calls and invitations no longer come his way, and he feels dead-ended at a time when he desperately needs an exit.

COMMON STRESS FACTORS

Mark, Dwight, and Ron represent many men in mid-life ministry. Obviously, and importantly, they each entered the ministry with a vision. All three have been consistent, dedicated, and to a certain extent, successful. Yet stress is taking its toll on their sense of fulfillment and motivation. By examining their common experiences, it is possible to isolate and explain some of the stress factors plaguing mid-life members of the clergy.

Family problems

The marital and family-life problems of many pastors mirror those found in the congregation. But the pastor, acting as a professional helper to his flock, is usually put on a pedestal—making it impossible for him to seek the help, counseling, and support that he needs as much as anyone. Feeling vulnerable and striving to maintain his credibility as a spiritual leader, the minister finds himself trying to ignore the reality of his problems or attempting to endure them in secretive, self-protective ways.

The pastor having difficulties with effective parenting is also vulnerable. Pastor Smith is under attack because his fifteen-year-old son is "resistant to his authority" and a "trouble-maker" in the teen group. Feeling his credibility as teacher and example somewhat shaken, Pastor Smith feels as though he lives in a glass house. The pressure of constant surveillance has become a key factor in the tension and the communication problems within his home. Observing no such pressure plaguing his peers, and bitterly resenting the double standard of which he is the chief victim, Pastor Smith's son understandably exhibits rebellious behavior.

Feelings of loneliness and isolation

One of the most common complaints of pastors and their wives is that they feel lonely within the community of believers. Now the laity may have some problem understanding how pastors, surrounded by large numbers of people, can possibly feel lonely; but it is true that frequently the minister isolates himself by adopting a rigid, traditional approach to the role of the minister. Operating with limited transparency or openness, which makes it difficult to build personal relationships, he makes his involvements with people so professionalized that he places himself in a social straight jacket. He has probably never learned how to build reciprocity into his relationships with others. Having entered the ministry with a deep hunger to be needed by others or to rescue others (a need or role reflecting his own family of origin), he finds it difficult to receive care for fear of being indebted to someone or for fear of being judged a failure, incompetent in some way.

It is not unusual for the pastor's wife to be more comfortable with spontaneous, open social communications than her husband. The pastor may perceive in other marriages no separation between the husband's professional life and his social life, so he cannot understand his wife's expressions of loneliness. For example, Harold is an extrovert. Able by force of personality to break into both the church community and the community at large, he is warmly received as a friend. But his wife, Martha, was raised in the home of a minister who demanded of his family strict adherence to the behavioral traditional roles. She finds herself overwhelmed by her husband's easy style and open manner. She is initially frightened by her husband's expectations of her, and she retreats from social gatherings that are informal and where it is unpredictable as to what is expected of her.

A related problem is that of isolation. Many pastors and wives have moved so often that they are disconnected from both their families of origin and any permanent social roots. It is extremely difficult to build lasting relationships if a person moves every three to five years, as many pastors do. The pastor who operates in isolation from other clergy may also be located some distance from a pastor of his own denomination. He may meet other pastors at conferences or retreats and find great support for a few days or hours, but soon he is required to return to the same sense of isolation and loneliness that has become an unsettling factor in his life. Recently I encountered many clergy who indicate that they are freer to build support group experiences with local clergy of other denominations than to rely on occasional communications with distant peers from their own denomination. The former relationship is more easily stripped of political maneuverings, unwanted competition, and the distraction of denominational programs and agenda.

The absence of "significant others" and support groups (open sharing and caring experiences with peers) is an ongoing problem for the pastor. Who will minister to him as he struggles with the tasks and crises of his own personal life? Who will provide the backup resources he needs when he becomes professionally overwhelmed? He may compound this problem by operating within a narrow, restrictive, secretive role, which many clergy do. Many people may see the minister more in his role rather than as a person "open" to them. It is not uncommon to find a pastor depicting his people as nonresponsive, when actually he has locked them out and thrown away the key to good communication. On the other hand, many pastors dare to be open and vulnerable to their congregations, only to be hurt by laymen incapable of relinquishing idealized images of the clergy.

Economic pressures

Whether he has taken the vow of poverty or not, the minister may discover that others have taken it for him. The following are commonly expressed feelings of pastors:

"The congregation has a double standard: one for the pastor and one for themselves."

"The parsonage stands as the major argument against any cost of living raise—a raise we feel we need in many other ways."

"I drive an old car that many of my congregation wouldn't consider driving, and yet I represent them to the community."

"I wish they would value the sacrifices of time and energy and commitment to care that are central to my ministry. When they lay the financial sacrifice on me I feel unappreciated."

"It isn't so much the money, as it becomes a symbol of how they feel about ministry in general and my ministry in particular."

The pastor's wife communicates similar reactions:

"There is so little we own that is truly ours. At times I long for the freedom of ownership in order to have the freedom to decorate the parsonage and truly express myself."

"My children dress less well than most of the children in the church."

"We have less adequate health care than we ought to have. If we ever face a family health crisis we will be devastated financially."

"I believe in sacrifice and dedication, too, but I believe God expects us to function as a community and to care for one another."

As these questions would indicate, many pastors' wives struggle with deep feelings of inadequacy and low self-esteem. Bringing traditional views of the role of women (homemaker, care agent) to a low-paying profession, the pastor's wife finds that the financial squeeze wreaks havoc on her self-image, often serving to drive her into postures of hostility and depression. One of the major problems permeating parsonages filled with marital and family-life conflicts is the pressure that the financial demands of life in the ministry places on close relationships.

Parish personalities

Every parish is unique! Individual personalities and their social and cultural experiences combine to form a unique blend of multifarious elements. A laity's history of experiences with prior pastors forms and to a certain degree formulates their expectations and perceptions of successive pastors. The attitudinal make-up of a pastor's congregation is either a source of great support to him in the fulfillment of his vision or a source of frustration and disappointment. For example, George Hendricks experienced three good, supportive congregations over a period of eighteen years of ministry. However, his experience in Craigville was unfortunate from the early days of his ministry there. He had always been given as much freedom as he needed to propose and implement his ideas and concerns in ministry, but now he encountered a strong church board which, through the leadership of one key member, thwarted George in a number of his initiatives. He now feels he took the excitement and affirmations of his last ministry into this parish and did not take enough time to build rapport and to survey the needs and perspectives of his present church community.

Yet his story is not that unusual. Mike Swenson was voted out of his church following twenty-five years of highly successful ministries in other communities. The chemistry between the pastor and the parish is a vital issue in placements, but often it is either not considered by leadership or a decision is based on inadequate processing of the facts. Most congregations have either a formal or informal process for evaluating ministerial candidates. These processes may include visitations, going to hear the candidate preach, and/or extensive interviews. But from the pastor's point of view, the lack of a reciprocal flow of information in the hiring process is frustrating and dangerous. Many pastors bring their own set of questions, based on their perspective of ministry and their concerns, about the readiness of that parish for the possible changes they might experience under his leadership.

The whole area of differences in role perspective operates as a major source of stress in the lives of clergy and family. Each congregation functions with its own complex set of mixed expectations. Some churches, holding ambivalent feelings about the amount and nature of the power they expect their pastor to wield, avoid this key issue during the trial visitation and/or interview. Then, when the pastor arrives to initiate his ministry, he is often confronted with a power structure completely different from what he had thought existed.

The twelfth chapter of First Corinthians preserves an essential ideal for the health of the congregation in its ministries. Paul proclaims, "For as the body is one, and hath many members, and all the members of that one body, being many, are one: so also is Christ" (v. 12). In reality both the pastor and people often find themselves running counter to this unifying principle that would build health and wholeness into the life of the church community. Perhaps a greater awareness is in order of both the differences that carry the potential to divide and the principles that free us to become whole in our ministries.

The tyranny of evaluation

The collective personality and informal political structure of the congregation is directly related to the issue of the pastor's accountability. Implicit in the tensions between clergy and congregation is the assumption that they are accountable to one another. The pastor's teaching and preaching ministries unite to emphasize their accountability to God, to the church, and often, by implication, to him. The congregation exercises both formal and informal methods of evaluating the pastor and communicating to him their perception of the quality of his ministry. That power of holding him accountable is an ongoing source of stress in the lives of many pastors and their families.

For instance, Phillip, a pastor's sixteen-year-old son, has been angry and withdrawn in recent months. He resists attending church and is beginning to establish primary ties with kids outside the church community. His father and mother have attempted to explore his feelings and perceptions; but when he began to criticize the church, they defended it and he retreated. Three months ago his father received an unfavorable vote—insufficient to remove him from the pastorate, but it was a clear communication of opposition and criticism. Phillip, always an admirer of his father, felt the people had been "unkind and unchristian." His identification with the church community had been undermined. He felt helpless when he tried to express his feelings to his parents.

In a similar case, Martha has struggled with depression during Charles' first year of ministry in Central Church. His prior church experience had been most unpleasant and he felt forced to resign following four years of ministry. Always functioning with enthusiasm and involvement, she now experiences much motivational difficulty in the present parish. Her health problems have become chronic and serve to excuse her from extensive participation in church life. Obviously, the impact of the negative church response on Charles has been significant. He seems to be motivationally "burned out." What he experienced in his past parish is negatively influencing his approach and perception of his present parish. The tyranny of evaluation is now undercutting the health and vitality of his marriage. Martha doesn't wish to unload her problems on him since he seems overwhelmed by church demands and problems; he tries to protect her from current tensions, having recognized how devastated she was by their last church experience. This tragedy reveals an all too familiar pattern:

a loss of communication resulting in a low quality of marital intimacy.

These two cases illustrate the tyranny of evaluation as it influences the pastor's family life. This tyranny of evaluation is also present in the pastor's relationship with the leadership of his denomination. While methods and procedures vary, the pastor is under the evaluative eye of his denomination. He is accountable to those who create and establish the programs, priorities, and goals for his ministry. I have found this to be more troublesome to some pastors than to others, depending on their individual identification with the political system of the church and their own sense of integrity within their ministry. Some pastors seem intimidated by evaluative procedures and authority, while other pastors view the leadership of the church as merely providing resources and options they feel free to use or to discard. Obviously the intentions of the evaluator, as well as the perceptions of the pastor, are crucial in sorting this out. Most pastors are open to the issue of accountability but many will resist what they consider to be unfair methods or means of implementation.

This tyranny of evaluation has an inner focus as well. The pastor brings his own expectations of himself into his ongoing ministry. Many pastors struggle with low self-esteem and are very hard on themselves, operating out of a severe or punitive sense of obligation. Therefore any evaluation done by others serves to trigger their own process of self-evaluation. It is difficult enough to measure up to the expectations of their own original vision, but their sense of what the local church and the denomination expect of them is frequently disheartening, if not devastating.

This tyranny often surfaces in pastor-peer relationships. What common words of greeting and conversation are overheard in a circle of clergy? The terms and usages are not unlike those of a group of businessmen. "How are you doing?" is either intended or interpreted to mean, "How is your church growing?" Often specific questions, evaluative by nature, are reciprocally asked: "How many did you have in church on Sunday morning?" "How is your Sunday school growing?" "Has the day-care center worked out?" Sometimes this noncommunicative "show and tell" becomes a poor substitute for real communication, and destroys both the atmosphere and opportunity for listening to lonely and troubled hearts.

On the other hand, many pastors find the informal and relaxed communications at conferences more helpful and healing than the formal agenda. Much of the initiative for escaping the tyranny of evaluation rests with the pastor himself. He must conscientiously avoid such surface evaluative communications and must build support group relationships that nurture more profound and meaningful communications. His own integrity in ministry will enable him to avoid intimidation by the evaluative procedures of others. Yes, the issue of accountability *is* an ongoing reality in everyone's life; but if the methods and criteria of evaluation become too legalistic, then the entire process becomes merely a source of isolation and estrangement. The curse of sin is the tyranny of legalistic evaluation; the victory found in grace builds love into both the nature and process of ministry. Perhaps the intangible nature of the minister's work makes the process of evaluation so complex and threatening. How does one objectively evaluate the quality of another's ministry? Roger Andrews has pastored a church through a period of major economic problems. Two factories had major lay-offs, affecting the job security of a large number of his congregation and forcing several families to move out of town. During one year he lost thirty-five people from his active membership. How can Roger be expected to abide by the evaluative criteria of others? Is it possible for others to comprehend the power of his ministry, to understand the constant care and sustaining love he showed to parishioners during periods of uprooting, loss, and change? This may have been the most important contribution he will ever make to a congregation. Roger himself must recognize that, seeing himself as accountable to God, and this enables him to function with great integrity in his ministry.

The absence of recreational balance

This intangible nature of his work also requires the minister to maintain a balance in his life. Yet I find pastors often overextending themselves, mistreating their bodies through neglect of healthy eating habits and having almost a complete lack of recreation. For example, Pastor James, having too high self-expectations and the resultant guilt, struggles with a weight problem. His eating, caused largely by anxiety-producing guilt, is unhealthy—if not physically self-destructive. Yet one of his enjoyments is eating, a behavior not only allowable and respectable but one that is actively reinforced. In addition, James can eat while working with and relating to his people. Therefore, like many pastors, he gives himself little room for relaxation and balance.

I find such pastors aware of the lack of balance in their lives, but they feel trapped within a set of values, priorities, and expectations that provide little chance for a shift in lifestyle. It is precisely this lack of balance in their lives which, when combined with the dilemma of accountability for intangibles, leads to physical "burn outs," perhaps even "nervous breakdowns." Most of us who work in intangible areas of endeavor enjoy working with our hands. We find fulfillment in viewing the sidewalk we laid, the wall we built, or the landscaping we designed and accomplished. Something concrete and measurable, the physical product of our own minds and hands, gives us more pleasure. No one can deny its existence or its practical value. Yet taking time for play may cause some to feel guilt. After all, aren't we supposed to put aside childish things? Whether it be at work or at play we must exercise, for when we neglect our bodies we pay the price with a health crisis or a collapse of motivation.

Motivational problems

The older the minister, the more likely that he will experience a motivational crisis. He has probably maintained a pace the average man would not be capable of. The resources of his vision and his faith have enabled him to maintain a high level of motivation for an extended length of time. As his early adult years terminate and his middle years approach, it becomes increasingly difficult for him to maintain that vision. All the above forces and stress factors, even though courageously resisted and handled, increasingly pressure him. As they crowd him, he may begin to reexamine his vision within the arena of ministry to human suffering. Often this confrontation with reality suggests that his anticipations of success in healing human hurt have not been realized. He may encounter some doubts about his ability to maintain that youthful vision with such limited reinforcement.

Motivational problems are signaled by some of the following symptoms:

- preoccupation and daydreaming
- inability to maintain attention in study
- procrastination in sermon preparation
- dread of committee and board meetings
- fear of or great resistance to visitation and calling
- spending extra time on meaningless peripheral activities that may be more identifiable or measurable
- extreme fatigue and restlessness

Many of these symptoms are related to a depression syndrome that may also include other difficulties such as:

- sleeping too little or too much
- eating too little or too much
- problems of sexual adjustment
- indecisiveness
- unrealistic guilt and remorse

When a pastor experiences many of the above symptoms he needs a good, thorough medical examination and possibly some counseling assistance to evaluate what is going on in his life. However, this process of self-evaluation becomes extremely threatening to the pastor because he feels as though he has failed twice. Not only has he failed to fulfill his own vision of the ministry, but he also seems to be a failure in his personal life. Tragically, this crucial time in the life of the pastoral minister often ends by his pulling the spiritual rug out from under his own feet.

Spiritual crises

The pastor is especially vulnerable to spiritual crisis because of the tremendous pressures placed on him to bring healing to the lives of so many broken people. This atmosphere of perpetual crisis subjects his ministry and his faith to constant testing and evaluation. Therefore, the above-mentioned stress factors may be difficult for him to confront since he may weigh them against his anticipated success and idealized self-image. His inability to accept his own deficiencies and needs in his earlier ministry may have isolated him from ongoing support group experiences. He may have assumed that he could "go it alone," be strong for everyone else, and "tough it out alone." Therefore, the motivational collapse directly connected with spiritual doubts and problems often comes at the very time he most needs his faith and his sense of God's presence. He has so focused on the problems and needs of others that he has failed to become the "child of the heavenly Father." His role has been to parent everyone and he finds it difficult to shift the focus. At this point he has lost contact with the words of the psalmist: "Out of the depths have I cried unto thee, O LORD . . . hear my voice" (Ps. 130:1). When he feels a failure in his ministry, he can rarely feel that God is present and blessing and accepting. Here is where he needs to relate to the words of the psalmist: "Yea, though I walk through the valley of the shadow of death (or depression) . . . thou art with me" (Ps. 23:4). When the vision hasn't been realized, it is easy to fall into the trap of questioning the content and validity of that vision in one's own experience.

THE INWARD FOCUS

Research into adult developmental tasks and crises reveals that during the mid-life phase there is an increasingly inward focus. New questions are asked about identity: who and how one will be and become. The clergy are clearly shaped by a combination of psychosocial forces and professional identity to focus on the "ins of it all." The origin of the pastor's call and his early adult expression of that vision have prematurely made the young pastor sensitive to the inward issues of life, the importance of the subjective self in relation to God. His professional life, with all its intense involvements with man's predicaments and hopes, continues to focus on internal subjective values and issues. The preaching ministry generally asks inner-directed questions: How may man struggle with sin? How may he hope for and achieve inner healing? The care and counseling of persons necessitates the clergy's constant contact with inner struggles and the dynamics of sin and sickness. No other calling is so consistently expressed in terms of this inward focus.

Due to this identification with the inward needs and struggles of others, it is easy for the layman to assume that the pastor has little personal difficulty with his own inward focus. Yet it is my experience that the clergy encounter the same basic tasks and crises in their psychosocial development as do the majority of their congregation. I would add that the pastor more readily and clearly identifies this development as a pilgrimage—the tasks, demands, and resources for response carry more definite spiritual questions and answers with them. But the basic human needs are the same.

The vast amount of reappraisal active during the middle years brings ongoing struggles with identity and, hopefully, increased self-awareness. Evaluation of one's past choices and examination of anticipated versus realized achievements receive much attention and frequently cause much tension. The pastor continues to relate his personal identity to his professional accomplishments. His vision has been a mixture of both. In the process of self-examination the pastor develops a new sense of self that establishes both a focus on who he has been and who he would like to become as a person and a disciple.

The first focus on who he has been and how effective he

has been may reveal painful inadequacies or failures along with the substantial achievements. But recognition of polarities in the Christian life enables the minister to see life and achievement more accurately in their "both/and" rather than "either/or" capacities. In *The Seasons of a Man's Life* the polarity between the *destructive* and *creative* urges as a very present reality to the person in mid-life passage is cited.[1] This is a powerful polarity in the personal and professional life of the pastor. Death and destruction are evident in man's estrangement, brokenness, and injustices. Because the pastor's vision thrusts him into the middle of this battle, he identifies with the apostle Paul that "we wrestle not against flesh and blood, but against principalities and powers in high places." He sees daily the works of those powers of sin and sickness engulfing the lives of those to whom he brings the word of hope.

Yet he also becomes increasingly aware of how he himself is personally ensnared in this polarity between destruction and creation. At times he identifies with Job and Jeremiah, crying out against the emptiness and hopelessness of man's puny struggles. At times he looks at his vision and the reality of his life and ministry and questions his own faith, stating, "My God, have You forsaken me, too?" This despair and doubt is compounded by an increasing awareness of his own humanness. He looks at the discrepancy between his vision of what man in faith might become and the reality of his own personal shortcomings. He remembers how often he preached a standard of human excellence that he himself has fallen short of in his dealings with people. He remembers the times he just couldn't handle the opposition any longer and became angry and unreasonable in conversation with a parishioner or a church board member. He has trouble allowing himself the right to have been so very human. Remembering how threatened he was when someone else was getting the recognition, he feels an utter failure in his ministry. This period spent in sorting out the disconnections between his idealism and his personal and professional experience need not become a period of disengagement. For some pastors it actually becomes a period of renegotiation and renewal. But, unfortunately, it all too often is accompanied by personal alienation and professional impotence.

Erikson sees the middle years as carrying the potential for "generativity and/or self-absorption and stagnation."[2] This potential is activated by the polarity mentioned above of destruction and creation in man's experiences and perspective of life. The self-destructive aspect of an individual withdraws from overt human contact and becomes self-absorbed. The resulting loss of interest in life causes an equal lack of motivation to serve. Some pastors, in desperation, even choose to leave the ministry. The "ins of it all" tell them that either they once made the wrong choice or else they cannot endure the polarities any longer. Others find that the process of reappraisal enables them to rediscover themselves—to find the ways, means, and internal strength to function more effectively as laymen. These clergy, while leaving the full-time ministry, have achieved a career reevaluation that is more of a redirection of service than a retreat from ministry. One such clergyman, Peter, had pastored for twenty-four years. During his early forties he began to face some of the problems of functioning as a pastor. He also discovered his problems handling opposition and criticism. By exploring these realities, he discovered that many aspects of his pastoral ministry—many of the overt problems—were a direct result of his own low self-esteem. This made him supersensitive to any evaluative measures. By confronting these internal dynamics, Peter became free to examine the nature of his original call. What surfaced was much evidence that the basis of his sense of being called was perhaps overcompensation for those intense feelings of inadequacy. As Peter dealt with these forces, he also became freer to look at his strengths, and how he might more effectively express them. This led to a decision to pursue further training in Christian education and work toward the goal of either teaching at the college level or working as a Christian Education Director for a church with a staff ministry.

Others demonstrate that they cannot accommodate the

polarities. They find it difficult to endure a reevaluative and reinvestment process so they allow the threat of leaving the security of the status quo to dominate them. They choose to not really choose. Quickly arriving at stagnation station, they function at a very low level of motivation and with some degree of depression. The pastor who chooses this road and arrives at this station exemplifies the person who has really (at least temporarily) given up on life. Henry David Thoreau calls attention to this state when he says in *Walden,* "The mass of men lead lives of quiet desperation. What is called resignation is *confirmed desperation.*"[3] The pastor who tells himself he is resigned to his lot is really operating out of what Thoreau later calls "a stereotyped but unconscious despair," and—layman or minister—"it is a characteristic of wisdom not to do desperate things."[4]

Arthur represents this process. He is now forty-eight years old and has been in his present parish for four years. It has been an uneventful ministry with little evidence of personal or professional growth. The church congregation has lost some of the initial excitement they had in his first year of ministry. Most of the peripheral members have drifted away and attendance has dropped steadily, to the point that some parishioners feel Arthur should begin to account for the loss. Arthur himself consistently avoids direct confrontations with his parishioners, retreating from many of his ministerial functions. He spends more time in the parsonage, creating some tensions with his wife who recognizes both his rapport problem with the people and his avoidance patterns. She sees him watching television during both the daytime and evening hours. She notices that his sermons are seldom written before late Saturday evening and then are hurriedly produced. She must constantly remind him that he needs to visit someone in the hospital or take care of a crisis in the parish. He has placed his wife in the position of negatively parenting him, which has served to undermine the nature and quality of marital intimacy.

While the physical changes of middle years are external

and quite obvious, it is the inward manifestation of this process that is most important. The physical changes inform the adult that time is passing and that youth and its opportunities are slipping away. Most researchers into the adult developmental process focus on the critical nature of physical change and its impact on the individual's sense of self and direction. Levinson notes that the word "young" represents "birth, possibility, initiation, openness, energy, potential. It colors the meaning we give to concrete images."[5] In contrast, "Old is a symbol representing termination, fruition, stability, structure, completion, death."[6] In both the clergyman's professional life of caring for people and in his own personal pilgrimage these symbols are powerful.

Frank initiated and maintained a most productive ministry during his thirties. He was particularly successful in attracting young people and had functioned as an associate minister to youth. At age thirty-eight he felt it was time for him to tackle a senior pastoral function. During his five years of ministry in this parish he has continued to be an effective minister to youth. Yet he seems intimidated by the middle adults and has received some open criticism for his lack of leadership in areas of administration and the care of older adults in the church. As you counsel with Frank you sense his strong identification with youth and also his resistance to his own personal aging process. His ineffectiveness in working with older adults seems to be related to his own problems with loss of youth and a lack of confidence with authority. He feels threatened by the partial disconnection from his own area of greatest effectiveness. At the same time he both feels and fears the personal and professional pressure to deal with other needs, tasks, and crises.

Frank has begun to question the choices he has made and like many men in the middle years is thinking about change. The tendency in such a crisis is to focus on a change of careers and/or wives. Frank struggles with both choices, causing him much anxiety and guilt. His fantasies relative to younger women in his parish are getting out of control and are troubling him deeply. The thought of a career change is connected to these fantasies in that he assumes it might free him from the pressures and guilt he is experiencing. Nancy Mayer states:

> Thus when a man in his middle years decides to burst constraining bonds for the sake of a dream, the decisive issue is self-awareness: whether or not he dares confront himself honestly and discard illusions about who he is. The man who runs away to avoid self-confrontation will discover that his geographic move is but a mirage.[7]

Assuming that Frank finds the support and counseling he needs, he may be able to confront the deeper problems with which he is struggling. His struggle with lost youth, lost identity, and loss of meaning in life reflects a significant spiritual crisis. This painful passage could become the basis for a profound personal pilgrimage.

The polarity of young and old suggests a theme that carries significant theological meaning for the pastor. He is engaged in a vocation that proclaims the hope of eternal life in the face of man's finitude. With the apostle Paul he in faith exclaims that this "mortal will put on immortality" (1 Cor. 15:53). Yet often the pastor himself becomes trapped in a merely terrestrial context for that hope. It is true that the quest for fame and recognition is not without its impact on the lives of clergy. In fact, one problem the pastor often reveals is a difficulty accepting the reality that he does at times function out of that motivation. Therefore, recognizing and confronting these dynamics of his own humanness become a significant part of his mid-life pilgrimage.

These polarities and tasks are generally encountered in the private and inner realm of being and becoming. However, they become manifest in the outward interpersonal realities of one's life. This is particularly true of the clergy who both personally and professionally experience these crises and tasks.

THE OUTWARD FOCUS

Ken is a highly ambitious and assertive pastor. His reputation as one who makes things happen was earned as he pastored five churches, all of which prospered. Two of them even underwent major building programs during his ministry. A fine preacher and always well prepared, he invested high levels of energy in all the functions of ministry. The administrative record leaves behind a testimony of his gift as an administrator. Somehow he finds the time and energy to call on people in crises and to maintain an effective hospital ministry. To all who observe or know him, Ken is a symbol of ultimate success in the ministry.

However, at the age of forty-eight Ken is struggling with some personal problems. He is the type of person who postpones seeking help since he is unable to risk personal vulnerability and exposure. After all, most of his energies are invested in demonstrating that he "has it all together." Some health problems and a doctor's strong recommendation that he endeavor to lower the level of stress in his life brought him in for counseling. He admits to feeling as if his time on this earth is limited—that he must push harder if he is to realize his goals for his life and ministry—and recently he has experienced a significant loss of energy. But Ken continues to drive himself, even while shouldering a load of fatigue. Fear of failure, which he confesses to, has been instrumental in his twenty-five years of overworking to prove himself competent. He has never been able to slow down or relax.

Ken has carried much of the conditional love experience of his early childhood into his adult life and ministry. He has always felt a deep need to prove himself worthy to others with whom he has any sense of intimacy. While preaching the gospel of love and grace, he operates as though he is justified by works. Ken represents what Friedman and Rosenman identify as the Type A personality, a type characterized by ambition and aggression: competition with oneself as well as others.[8] Ken tends to undertake many projects simultaneously, usually excelling in them all. When at home he works; thus the family plays a limited part in his life. It is in this dimension of his life that Ken is currently reaping the harvest of neglect.

The outward focus of the pastor's life (the way he handles his external affairs) is intricately related to the way in which he handles the intimacies of his personal and professional experience. Getting professionally established while in his twenties should leave him freer to develop within himself—now a successful pastor—a strong sense of family and community; but the outward demands of his role in the ministry often create tension between him and his family, making it difficult for him to build family roots and meet their needs. Marriage, family, and community intimacies become more critical to the pastor in his thirties. There is often a good deal of guilt and anger in his experience when he fails to fulfill these tasks, particularly since he often preaches to these issues. As he enters his forties he is forced to reevaluate the way in which he has responded to the intimacies of his life.

To put it simply, Ken has neglected his wife and his children. His success in building church community experiences has enabled him to avoid a clear confrontation with his failures on the home front. Now that his children are into their teens and exercising their independence, the gulf between him and his children has widened, undercutting both his authority and their trust in his love. While the children often display a degree of admiration and identification with his success, they also show a marked hostility toward the church. The latter emanates from their feeling that the church and its demands kept their father from them. Therefore, the oldest boy, Michael, refuses to attend church, and upon graduating from high school disappointed his parents by not going to a church-related college. Michael has now reversed roles, becoming remote and indifferent even as his father was to him.

The task of helping one's children cope with their needs and responsibilities is central to adult life during the middle years. Erikson sees this as a part of the process called generativity: i.e., becoming creatively involved in assisting the next generation to become whole and fulfilled persons.[9] Pastors and their wives often invest a majority of their time, energy, and financial resources fulfilling this task. However, many pastors invest so much of themselves in this process that their own children feel great pressure to produce and perform. Feeling accountable for their behavior and vulnerable to the critical perspective of the parishioners, the pastor often makes his children feel an unfair pressure to conform, which often leads to their rebellion. This paradox of intention is one of the major problems encountered as one counsels with parsonage families. The great emotional investment of parents in the lives of their children is perceived by the child as parental over-control or overprotection—evidence of mistrust.

Generally, we find parsonage families quite healthy. Even when problems of independence and control do exist, they are usually perceived by both parent and teen-ager as extensions of the role expectancy dynamics of the parsonage experience. Most so-called "P.K.'s" (preacher's kids) articulate and demonstrate high levels of respect for their parents and their values. This usually follows the successful completion of the task of independence and the fulfillment of young adult tasks, without the pressures of the nuclear family unit within the context of a demanding community climate.

The pastor and wife, who would fulfill this task of assisting their teen-age children to become, also need to let go and trust. One of the related problems I encounter with parsonage families is the mix of high-level expectation and guilt on the parents' end of the process. I think of the case of Mark and Linda who raised their four children, only to discover that three of them were outside of the church by the time they were in their thirties. While parental communication patterns and expectations were in part related to this dilemma, the picture was really far more complex. The choices of the children were significantly related to their perceptions of the treatment of the family by the church communities in which the behavior of the parsonage kids was often unfairly critiqued.

The parents' anxiety over maintaining rapport and respect in the church added great stress to how the family dealt with the normal issues of adolescent identity and independence. Much of their rejection of the church comes out of the rejection they experienced as adolescents in the church. Unfortunately, the parents' preoccupation with their own failures served to complicate communication and reconciliation. Perhaps the major negative influence imposed by the parents was their negative and cynical communication about the church in the presence of their children. While there was much reality to support their communications, it has only served to make renegotiation of a relationship with the church very difficult for their children.

Virginia Satir asserts that behind a dysfunctional family you will often find a dysfunction in the marital relationship, although this problem in the marital relationship may not surface as long as the children are in the home. It has been in, through, and around the lives of their children that many couples maintain a semblance of marital communication. During the middle years the children are attaining independence, and as each one leaves, it is as though another protective layer is removed, exposing unresolved tensions and conflicts in the marital relationship. Havighurst identifies the task of "relating to the spouse as a person"[10] as typical of the middle adult years. Perhaps the children and all of the related tasks and crises of raising them have separated Tim and Jennifer. As the last child leaves, the home takes on the quality of an empty shell with loneliness and isolation felt. Communication patterns have to be established and/or renegotiated. Parents may discover that they have some unresolved role expectancy problems and do not have a solid pattern of communication for resolving these. Tim has difficulty confronting the anxiety and depression that have become more pronounced in Jennifer as the children have departed. It has become clear that the children had served to meet her need for companionship and meaningful intimacy; now she feels that Tim has locked her out and is too preoccupied with his own life and ministry to relate to her. As she talks about going back to college and pursuing a career, he withdraws in anger. Somehow he sees her as declaring that he has failed or that their marriage is not enough for her. She responds with feelings of resentment over his double-standard treatment of their respective needs and goals. They have been through a period of high-level stress due to a combination of these problems and their resistance to seeking help. Like so many couples in the ministry with marital tensions, they fear the loss of face that they assume to be involved in seeking help.

Levinson identifies another polarity in the experience of mid-life as involving the tension between being *masculine* and *feminine*. [11] The divisions of labor and the place of ambition are a part of this process. The changing role of men and women is affecting the parsonage couple as well. Sometimes it is the economic pressures that thrust the woman back into the work world, while in other cases it relates to her quest for meaning and purpose as the children leave. Nevertheless, the impact of the change is being felt. Some men in the ministry find it most difficult to harmonize their own idealism with the realism of having these changes occurring in their own lives. I think of Harold who would be identified as a strong advocate of minority rights and one who often raises a prophetic voice relative to injustices in the community. Yet Harold is having a major marital crisis in his early fifties. His wife has become increasingly independent and active in her own career, which has placed him under considerable pressure to share roles and functions in the home. It has awakened much self-confidence in her and he finds her ambition to be difficult to relate to now. He is discovering that much of his prophetic preaching and professional participation in areas of human rights is not easily related to his own marital relationship. He clearly dominated the marriage and the family for twenty-six years. This gave him much freedom and a feeling of integrity that is now somewhat shaken by changing roles and expectations in the family and marriage.

A major task of the middle years is supposed to be the development of leisure time activities. Pastors tend to function more like the corporation executive who has trouble slowing down during these years of his life. He has developed a routine lifestyle and pattern of behavior that is difficult to change. For most, the professional life has become the primary focus of identity, and it becomes difficult to build leisure time into one's lifestyle. Ideally this would be happening as the children become independent, freeing the pastor and his wife to build new interests and activities into their relationship. This would serve to increase his coping capacity with the stress of the ministry. Unfortunately, many clergy fail to take this opportunity to enrich the quality of intimacy and their own health and vigor for life and ministry.

Another dimension of this outward focus is the broader and more varied qualities of intimacy and generativity available in community. The clergy again cope very well with this task and are facilitators and key resource people for the building of community. Levinson identifies the polarity of attachment and separation as another task confronting the middle-aged male. He notes that, "To be attached is to be engaged, involved, needy, plugged in, seeking, rooted. Attachment in this sense is a general condition that has many sources and takes many forms."[12] The pastor is keenly aware of this dynamic in the lives of those to whom he ministers. He sees the church as the community of faith, providing an answer to the loss of the extended family, and the absence of a support group in the lives of so many people. Yet, as was noted, the research on stress in the ministry identifies loneliness as a key problem reported by both clergy and their wives. While professionally aware and influential in this area, he may suffer from private feelings of detachment, lacking a sense of rootedness. The pastor who moves frequently will likely experience the sense of limited attachment as he enters the middle years and sees his family grow up and leave. He and his wife may be removed by great distances and time from their families of origin. It is one thing to understand this need and to minister to others; it is another thing to deal with it in one's own personal life.

Yet separation, too, has its place in the middle years. The capacity to handle solitude and to take the journey inward is crucial to these years. Clergy are generally both gifted and prepared in dealing with the polarity of attachment and separation. They generally know how to love and to be deeply attached, and also how to separate and meditate.

The Upward Focus

We have addressed ourselves to the ins and outs of it all. The tasks and needs for both inward journeys and outward commitments are continuous realities in the development and pilgrimage of the adult. At times they complement and interrelate. At other times they are polarized and add stress to the process of growth. There is another dimension that compounds all this and that has to do with the *ups of it all.*

There are two important factors operating in this upward focus for the clergy. The task of advancement for the person in his thirties and the reevaluation of his dream in the forties and fifties is both like and dissimilar to the same process in the lives of others. These tasks have both kingdom of man and kingdom of God forces operating in the life of the clergy. Their own aspirations and need for success combine with their commitments and sense of accountability to God. This is clearly a significant difference in the lives of clergy compared to the processing of these tasks in the lives of other people in their middle years. Confronting and resolving this polarity is a critical task for clergy in the middle-life period.

The pastor in his forties and fifties will take a new look at the vision he has pursued over the past twenty or more years. It may be done so privately, and in such isolation and loneliness, that few recognize this process. The pastor often feels the lack of support systems or significant resource people and goes it alone. The process may show up in the content of his preaching, which expresses his reevaluation of the vision in relationship to the failures of the institutional church. This may lead him into some radical decision-making such as leaving the ministry, changing churches, or establishing new priorities in his ministry.

As noted earlier, he may drift into the middle years as though there were no new tasks or crises. However, that very process may reveal that he is making a choice. It is the passive-aggressive choice or the response of apathy and indifference. He has arrived at what may become stagnation station. The vitality and creativity that fed into his early vision for ministry may have burned off. The tests of time and role experimentation in actual ministry suggest to him that he doesn't have it or that the realities of life in the church have thwarted the realization of his vision. The depression potential in losses is an important reality in the experience of many clergy. The high idealism of the young adult years may have run out. The motivation that carried him into his early ministry was not sufficient to maintain him when other tasks and demands for his own new phase of developmental experience surfaced.

Donald found his middle to late thirties to be the most stressful period of his life and ministry. He felt caught in the middle of the ins, outs, and ups of it all. The pursuit of the vision, the tasks of meeting marital and family needs, and the pressures of achievement had become increasingly demanding in those years. A highly motivated and success-oriented man, he experienced much frustration over having to meet the domestic demands, while aspiring to fulfill a vision that seemed to be slipping away. While advancement and success may serve to complement marital and family needs for security, the time and energy invested may create relational vacuums during those critical years. It is difficult to manage the establishment of roots and the realization of vision-related goals. Donald feels that he lost his opportunity for a "successful ministry" due to all the other demands and "distractions" during those years. He is now into his middle forties and realizes that he has greater freedom than he had during those years. His two children have finished college and are on their own. His wife has focused some new interests in education and service at this point in her life. This has become a time for him to reexamine his vision and to sort out some new options for life and ministry. He is much more keenly aware of time factors in his life. There is an edge of panic and excitement about exercising this "one last opportunity."

There are powerful internal and external demands for achievement and advancement throughout the young adult and early middle-life years. A major task becomes focused during these middle years, which involves settling some basic questions about his vision, his goals, and for what and to whom he will be accountable. While there are those who come up with either answers of apathy or radical change, others settle for more creative alternatives. This is what Erikson means by the power of generativity in the middle years, expressed through care for community and the next generation. No other vocation better prepares a man for this task than does the ministry, since the pastor has been expressing this process throughout his professional life. This gives him a significant advantage in confronting the related personal tasks. The accountability dynamics are shifting from self-imposed and societal norms for success toward the Author of the vision who has also promised to enable His disciple to fulfill that call. This is why the passage of mid-life becomes a positive pilgrimage in the life of the pastor. The upward focus is primarily on the enabling power of God's love and grace working in all the expressions of the pastor's personal pilgrimage.

4

Senior Years in Ministry: Dreams to Live By

Dreams represent the process of integrating the past and the present as a basis for hope in the future. Time builds a reservoir of experience, and during the process it is the future that pulls man toward that which he truly values. Man seldom enters into the now of his experience with a freedom from the drag of the past and the pull of the future. During the transition years of the sixties there is a deep sense of time distortion as the past, present, and future interrelate, overlap, and complement. These are years of transition and termination, but they are also years that carry the potential for the renewal of one's integrity in hope, with dreams to live and die by.

At age sixty-two, Douglas is pastoring a congregation of fewer than one hundred members. While he has felt dead-ended during the last five years of his ten years in the parish, no other opportunities have arisen to quicken his motivation or optimism. At times he feels that his congregation wishes he would make a move, and they fear that he may hang on until retirement. Money has been a recurring problem throughout his ministry but this is now felt more acutely, due to his wife's recent health problems. She has also suffered with depression problems and is pressuring him to take an early retirement, on the basis that she cannot manage what she perceives as her role as "a good pastor's wife." He doesn't know how they will manage even if they wait until he is sixty-five for retirement, since his social security and ministerial pension are very inadequate. They own no property and have no significant amount in savings, and the earlier he retires the sooner they will confront these unpleasant realities. They do have three children with families of their own and may have to turn to them for assistance at that time. A life of ministering to others in time of need is in transition toward major personal needs and crises.

Edgar has always been an active and productive person and is about to retire from the ministry. While he could stay on in this present parish assignment until age seventy, he has been experiencing some serious blood-pressure problems which his work pattern complicates. His wife is positively anticipating their retirement for two reasons. First, she has never felt too fulfilled in the ministry and has resisted what she perceives as the expected role of the pastor's wife. Second, she is very dependent on him and has a deep and realistic fear that something will happen to him if he continues on in the ministry. Edgar has mixed feelings about retirement, having a sense of his health crisis and an awareness that retirement may not slow him down so much as frustrate him to the point of irritation and restlessness. He experiences much disappointment when he contemplates giving up the functions of the ministry which are so woven into his identity and purpose in living. He has considered taking on an associate role that might meet his need for continuity in the transition years, but which would not meet his wife's needs. He is also aware that he would have trouble being accountable to a younger man in the ministry, particularly since he himself has trouble delegating responsibility and has always held on to authority and control.

Tom is planning on retirement in six months when he

will turn sixty-five. He knows he will have many adjustment problems in dealing with this period of transition and termination. His present parish has provided him with one of his most fulfilling ministries, in which he is a warmly respected pastor and has established solid professional relationships within this community of twenty thousand people. He feels that it was here, during his last eight years of ministry, that he settled many personal and professional issues that had blocked his freedom in the earlier years of his ministry. He and his wife, Marjorie, have a retirement cottage in another state nearer their children and grandchildren, but they feel less drawn there than they did several years ago. Should he stay in this community when he retires and how will his congregation and his successor feel about this? In Tom's case, an associate role is a more viable option than it is for Edgar, since he has fulfilled most of his age appropriate tasks and has dealt with issues of authority and control effectively. One problem he anticipates is that his successor might not choose to have him continue on, and it may well be that the rapport he has built with the community in general will make it difficult for his successor. Another related option would be to establish such a role in another parish and community and draw on his strengths to build the same kind of rapport he has established here. Whatever the choices he makes, one has the feeling that Tom will cope well with the transitions and terminations.

CHANGING ELEMENTS AND LOSSES

The experiences with transition of these three men represent some of the tasks and crises confronting pastors in the senior years of their ministries. Each of these three men has had good years of human service, and their care for others has often been directed at the age and phase of life they are now entering. They have counseled and cared for families dealing with these difficult transitions and crises. What has been so central in their professional activities is now confronting them personally. While this has given them some basis for preparation, they are discovering that there are preparations that were neglected and that the struggle of the transition and termination years is inevitably bound up in the cycle of life. For the man in the ministry, one would expect that it would carry much potential for the hope of a pilgrimage process with dreams to live and die by.

Physical changes

One of the major changing elements during these transition years involves the many dimensions of physical change. While such changes are continuous throughout life, the loss dynamics surface most dramatically during these years—involving health loss, energy loss, mobility loss, acuity loss, and appearance loss (see Fig. 2). Such changes and losses occur irrespective of persons or their roles in society. While the clergy are more likely to have perceived the realities of the temporal and finite, this may have led some into patterns of neglect that undercut their readiness for coping with the changing elements and losses. This is well illustrated by the great number of pastors who neglect their physical health in the process of ministering to others and then confront declining health and all the related losses at this senior life phase. Such neglect now complicates their capacity to maintain their priorities. The very nature of ministry lends itself to the care of others and the neglect of oneself. This becomes apparent in the pastor who physically burns out in his middle years and suffers with a major heart attack in his later years. The incidence of cardiovascular difficulty in the ministry suggests that this pattern is not uncommon. The commandment to "love your neighbor as yourself" is not effectively translated by the pastor into his personal health care. Pastors often refer to the scriptural charge, "Know ye not that your body is the temple of the Holy Spirit!" (1 Cor. 6:19). They effectively relate this to matters of moderation and abstinence and yet neglect their own nutrition and exercise. Problems with eating and weight control seem to be acceptable exceptions to the above principles.

RETIREMENT TRANSITIONS

Changing elements	*Losses*
A. Physical changes	1. Health loss
	2. Energy loss
	3. Mobility loss
	4. Acuity loss
	5. Appearance loss
B. Environmental changes	1. Job loss
	2. Role or function loss
	3. Home loss
	4. Economic loss
C. Social and cultural changes	1. Family loss
	Children
	Spouse
	Extended family
	2. Social group loss
	3. Community loss

Figure 2

At a recent conference involving fifty pastors I asked them to indicate whether or not they had a balanced and continuous recreational or exercise routine. Only one young man, out of that entire group, was able to claim such a program. Many of the men reported great difficulty with their priorities in this area and in fact felt guilty over taking "time to play." The failure to play leads to negative health payoffs in later years.

Energy loss is a common crisis in the senior adult years, particularly problematic to the one who demands more of his body than he ought to. The above physical neglect carries serious consequences for energy loss and creates a vicious cycle, unless a major change in prioritizing and lifestyle occurs. This is illustrated in the case of Edgar, who is trapped by health, and who copes with problems in both himself and his wife. In his case the motivation for ministry is weakened, yet he is forced to function for economic and related reasons.

The loss of sensory acuity is a major adjustment problem for the individual engaged in human service activities. The pastor depends on his visual capacity in both his preparation and service activities. His listening skills are crucial to his ministries of visitation, care, and counseling. Most of these losses can be compensated for through good medical treatment and balanced living. The pastor who fails to take care of his health, nutrition, and exercise pays a price for that neglect.

The loss of one's mobility is a major adjustment for many senior citizens and can undercut one's involvement in a demanding ministry. However, the older pastor who is willing to make the transition into an associate role may be able to maintain some significant level of fulfillment and effectiveness in ministry. The readiness of his church to support and encourage such transition adjustments is an important consideration. While other institutions are beginning to provide opportunities for those nearing retirement age to maintain full-time employment, the church has historically been open to this. However, it needs to be added that there are denominational exceptions and that local churches vary considerably, depending largely on their own experiences with older pastors. In some cases it is clear that the institutional church has bought into the youth emphasis and has failed at this point in that it has neglected the great wealth of talent and wisdom possessed by older clergy.

Environmental changes

It becomes apparent that the physical change elements are interrelated with environmental changes. For most retirees there is the initial adjustment to job loss and related role and function changes. Most men report major adjustment problems at this point in their lives due to the fact that such a large percentage of their lifetime has been invested in the world of work. Even if they look forward to retirement, there are major demands for adaptation to time and space changes. The pastor experiences this same process, compounded by the fact that so much of his work experience involves critically important functions in the lives of others. His role has provided him with a degree of recognition as well as the stress of mixed and contradictory role expectations and stereotypes. The transition into retirement involves some painful terminations and loss.

Whether or not the pastor owns his own home, he usually confronts the task of relocation at this point in his ministry. As we examine the social and cultural changes, this will be seen as quite complicated. The question of environmental roots is a difficult one for pastors to deal with at retirement. Environmental roots for some are in the distant past and may be different for the husband and wife. The absence of continuity of environmental experience is compensated for by the reality that pastors and wives generally have learned how to adjust to changing environments and to cope very successfully with them. The major problem is economic in nature. The loss of job and home may combine with inadequate retirement planning, leading to much transitional difficulty for pastors.

Social and cultural changes

Ask a clergyman where home is, and you will find that many have difficulty clearly answering that question. For some it connects with an earlier and more successful long-term parish experience. The present parish may be, as it was for Tom, a most desirable location for retirement but with significant issues and complications to be resolved.

The pastor has likely established his professional and personal sense of community through one of the following:

his own parish

his involvement in the larger community

his fellowship with clergy associates of other denominations

his pastoral relationships within his denominational conference, district, or area

In most instances, he has a far more rich and vital sense of community than most who are approaching the terminations of roles and functions of their senior years. His major problem in his retirement frequently involves terminations with these resources and a transition to some earlier determined place for retirement. Thus the senior pastor in the ministry confronts the major task of establishing a sense of community on retirement. Some pastors and wives select retirement communities sponsored by their own denomination which they view as providing them with continuity of tradition, experience, and values system. Whatever the option selected, this phase of life brings confrontation with uprootings and reinvestments.

PATTERNS OF ADAPTATION TO RETIREMENT

The adaptive potential of older people has become a subject of increasing interest and research. While patterns or styles of adaptation are becoming identified, it is also evident that there is a richness and variety to these patterns, depending on everything from the minister's earlier psychosocial history to his present health and resources. The clergy, as a group, are unique inasmuch as their primary sense of identity and role has involved them in human service and community, inclusive of the adjustment needs and crises of the senior citizen population. Their personal adjustment to these transition years are significantly influenced by these functions. Robert Atchley reviews three approaches that have been identified in studying the adaptive process of older people: disengagement, substitution, and consolidation. These approaches help us grasp what is going on in the lives of clergy entering the retirement years.

Dimensions of disengagement

The process of disengagement is the separation of the individual from society through either self-chosen or socially determined terminations of role or functions. This style of adaptation generalizes from these terminations to a pattern of withdrawal from society both personally and professionally. The pastor has little inclination to select this as a viable option. His identity has been so connected with his role and functions in society that there is generally a search for some continuity of engagement. As Atchley notes, "An older person who is very active, in the sense of interacting frequently with people, may simply be a disengaged person searching for a new identity."[1]

Some pastors pursue this pattern of passage into retirement. I think of Phillip, who survived some difficult years of transition, including two successive pastoral assignments that involved much polarization with parishioners over their expectations and his performance. His wife's declining health and his own decreased energy and motivation left him vulnerable to criticism at the very time he most desperately needed support. In his earlier years in ministry he had encountered some difficulty with power struggles in his churches but generally managed to "win the struggles." These earlier patterns are surfacing much more powerfully now at the time of his transition into retirement. He also complains of a lack of denominational support and upon retirement has entered a period of disengagement. His termination of pastoral role and functions was soon followed by a pattern of minimal church involvement as they moved into a retirement community. Even within that community there has been little evidence of investment in building new relationships. Perhaps the disengagement is easier than the continuing reminder of failure and disappointment he experiences while participating in the church. Yet there is a breakdown in the integrity of his life and ministry that privately troubles him. It is likely that some process of reinvestment will occur before too long, but he is not likely to evidence any dramatic new engagement.

The process of disengagement varies from person to person, and in some instances represents a greater degree of investment in matters of the soul. Atchley states that:

> With each withdrawal from a role, the individual becomes increasingly preoccupied with himself or herself. Gradually the individual equilibrium achieved in middle age and oriented toward society is replaced through the process of disengagement by a new equilibrium centered around the individual's inner life in old age.[2]

While this could reveal a positive approach to the senior years, the danger is that it may represent self-pity and self-absorption that leads only to despair and cynicism. The positive emphasis on the inner life in old age is a focus that becomes important to the process of coping with the changing roles and declining capacities of old age. The clergy are well prepared for these years since the focus of their personal and professional existence has been on the quality of the inner life and the pursuit of matters of the soul.

Functional substitutions

As Atchley points out, "When people lose certain roles or the capacity to perform certain activities, an obvious way of adapting is to find a substitute."[3] This depends on a number of factors inclusive of the capacities of the individual, his financial security, and his options for selection.

Mark Jacobs planned for his retirement years by maintaining some avocational interest in ceramic and wood craft creations. Upon retirement he invested much time and energy in these endeavors and has discovered some new opportunities for fulfillment and social involvement. He operates a small gift shop and teaches a class in adult education at the local high school. His active participation in the senior adult fellowship of a local church provides him with spiritual and social resources.

Henry Martin was forced into an early retirement due to a major heart attack at the age of sixty-one. During the past several years he has developed a strong interest in stamp collecting and in buying and selling antique books. He approaches these activities at a leisurely pace and has established a significant network of new and interesting relationships with people in his town. He and his wife visit many old churches and have both discovered some fascinating old books and built rich fellowship into their retirement years.

Roger Foster concluded a long and successful career in the ministry, including a period of denominational leadership. As his health declined he was forced to adjust to limited energy and mobility. It was at this time in his life that he pursued his interest in becoming a ham radio operator and developed a large network of contacts with people, leading to the exchange of postcards and ongoing communication. This became a rewarding way for him to spend much of his time.

Consolidation of commitments

Another approach to old age is to accept the terminations and limitations but also to consolidate activities and energies that need not be surrendered or lost. Due to their generally solid academic background and extensive involvements with human service, the clergy have many options for consolidation. Andrew is a fine example of effective consolidation, having faced retirement in advance, seeking placement as a part-time associate pastor for visitation. He was able to pace himself and approach these pastoral care activities in a leisurely manner, which enabled him to build significant rapport with people. He is a much-loved and respected member of the church and enjoys a special relationship with the shut-ins affiliated with the church. Like Andrew, many pastors find this approach of consolidation to be very effective in dealing with their own needs at this time of life.

However, there are limitations to this for some men in the ministry. Atchley has cautioned that "consolidation may also not be a satisfactory solution if the lost activity was extremely important to the person's life and the remaining activities, though perhaps plentiful, are not able to serve as the basis for a meaningful life."[4] Jason Smith encountered this as he, like Andrew, tried some part-time associate roles in the church. He found himself increasingly preoccupied with his loss of functions as he observed the younger man in the ministry doing what he had done in the past. He found himself being critical of the style and pace of this younger man, soon realizing that this was neither a healthy situation for them nor for the church. In Jason's situation it became apparent that a substitution approach was the most workable adjustment, so he retired from the ministry. While maintaining a rich spiritual fellowship with a fine church community, he picked up his long-neglected interest in American history and took an active role in the historical association of the town to which he retired.

It is my observation that retired clergy tend to have a rich and diversified approach to these options for adaptation. While there are those who clearly demonstrate one of these three patterns, there are many who evidence a combination, moving through periods of consolidation to substitution to disengagement. Whatever the pattern or sequence, most clergy experience this passage period as a pilgrimage, demonstrating the power of integrity in their senior years.

PSYCHOSOCIAL PROCESS AND THE PILGRIMAGE

The style or approach of the pastor to the tasks and crises of these years is significantly influenced by both his personal psychosocial history and his professional experiences (see Fig. 3). The fulfillment of the tasks and crises of life leads to the experience and expression of integrity in accepting one's life as it has been. For the pastor, one's life and service is viewed from the perspective of God's ordination and blessing.

The capacity to trust is one of the most important strengths a person brings into these later years. The pastor who has built his life and ministry on the trusting power of faith enters his senior years with integrity and hope. Trust in its larger theological meaning is identified as faith, which is the foundation stone upon which one builds a pilgrimage into the psychosocial processes of living and serving. This is not to say that pastors do not struggle with elements of mistrust and despair. For some, the earlier and unresolved experiences with mistrust may surface again as the focus shifts from service in behalf of others to retirement adjustments and the related losses.

Martin Henderson had maintained an effective ministry in spite of occasional problems with mild depression. His own childhood was marked with difficult adjustment problems and unhappy family relationships. His parents divorced when he was ten years old, leaving his highly anxious and overworked mother to raise five children. His father's alcohol problems and

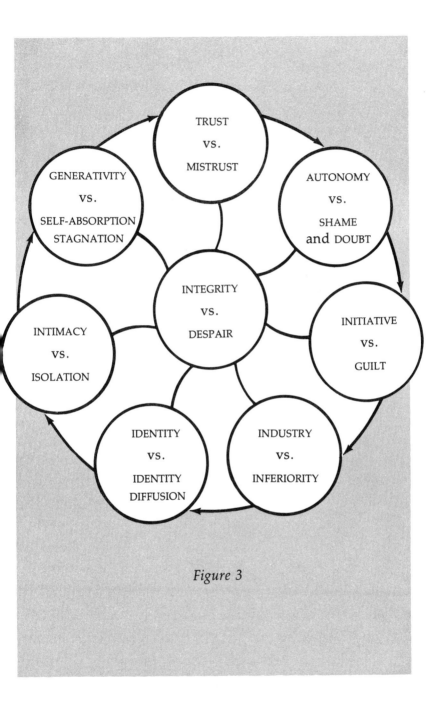

Figure 3

abusive communication pattern left deep elements of mistrust in the lives of the children. Martin's mother began to bring the children to church when he was fourteen, leading to a conversion experience shortly thereafter. This helped Martin to resolve his past anger and guilt and provided him with a sense of community and identity. It was on this foundation that he developed a sense of God's call for him to serve the less fortunate members of society. His ministry revealed great capacity for compassion and effectiveness in responding to the needs of his parish. Yet he admits to having continuing difficulty in receiving from others.

The loss of his role as pastor was a major adjustment crisis for Martin, leaving him mildly depressed, restless, and indecisive. The adjustment demands of these years, combined with the loss of role, left him vulnerable to the old scars of mistrust. It is critical that men like Martin be given every possible opportunity to maintain some channels for ministry in their senior years.

The capacity to be autonomous is an important part of integrity since it provides the strength necessary to explore the new tasks and opportunities of retirement years. When combined with initiative, the individual does not shrink back in defeat but confronts retirement in creative ways. The pastor is often called on to make some major decisions and moves upon retirement, and will need to develop a new sense of community and personal fulfillment. Whether he adopts a style of substitution or consolidation, it demands the strengths of trust, autonomy, initiative, and industry. Most pastors have a significant advantage at this basic level of adjustment. The principles and purposes he has lived by are maintained even when external circumstances change. The shrinking boundaries of temporal affairs and functions are confronted with his primary sense of a pilgrimage, leading him to new depths of spiritual awareness and meaning.

Identity for the clergy is a complex mix of personal psychosocial experience and professional life expression. The minister may have avoided dealing with the identity issues of late adolescence and young adult years. If his vision were more form than content, then the loss of role in these senior years may reawaken the unresolved identity confusion and manifest itself in despair. Ministerial duties and functions and parish activities may have become so much the focus of his life that he continued to avoid the question of identity. Now, as these external props are lost, the old issues confront him again with the added reality that time is running out. However, if these roles, functions, and responsibilities were structures or means of expressing a deep sense of identity and discipleship, that continuity of identity enriches these years. The vision that was truly whole and holy enables the older man to dream dreams with integrity.

Intimacy is a primary theme in the life of the pastor who proclaims the power of God's love as the answer to man's estrangement, loneliness, and isolation. No other vocation addresses itself with such breadth and depth in presenting this concept. The integrity of a person in old age is keyed to his sense of the truth he has lived by. The Christian concept of grace enriches the meaning of integrity beyond that of the mere acceptance of one's own life. The pastor sees his life as "in Christ" and his vocation as "blessed of God." He is enabled to accept having been, on the basis that what he has done is an expression of a pilgrimage of faith.

The concepts of newness and the new life in Christ represent the ongoing reality that for the Christian all things continue to become new, even in old age. There have been painful struggles in the process of wrestling with life's tasks and demands, but the man of God pursues this process as a pilgrim. The descent has not been without its ascent, nor the pain without purifying power. Of all the professions, the ministry stands out as in touch with man's questions and God's answers. He affirms that "Love knows no limit to its endurance, no end to its trust, no fading of its hope; it can outlast anything. It is, in fact, the one thing that still stands when all else has fallen."[5]

The pastor emeritus is a concept that holds significant

meaning for the community of faith. It represents a strong statement of positive valuation of the senior men in ministry in the face of the world's perceptions and persecution. As was noted earlier, the pastor is often stereotyped by the secular society and the media as weak or naive and his message as irrelevant. It is tragic that sometimes this attitude carries over into the way in which the church treats her ministers. A great untapped resource we have are these men of the pilgrimage perspective. All too often we have forced them into disengagement without support and have undermined their potential to enrich our lives. They carry such a rich reservoir of depth and breadth experiences with man's questions and God's answering responses. They are our vessels of honor and should not be forced into isolation and stagnation. Young men and women seeking direction for living and serving need to know the mentoring power of these men who have gained the pilgrimage perspective. Accepting his life and ministry as ordained and blessed of God, he "dreams dreams" and passes on to the next generation the promise that "your young men shall have visions."

5

Pressures, Priorities, and Renewal

We have explored the tasks, needs, and crises confronting the pastor as he journeys through the young adult years, confronts the mid-life transitions, and encounters the senior years of his life. The very fact that he acknowledges these realities and accepts the tension between the human element and the Christian ideals enriches his potential for ministry. He is touched by the same pressures, struggles, and powers as those to whom he ministers. While some might put him on a pedestal, thinking him invulnerable, and others might stereotype him as naive and uninformed, the reality is that he brings experiences into his ministry that extend his authority and enrich his capacity to care and communicate. The combination of dealing with the human element in his own life, while through faith experiencing it as a pilgrimage, gives him significant credibility in responding to the needs of others.

Unfortunately, the pastor is often deprived of the very ministry he himself needs. That old proverb recurs and rings in his ears, "Physician—pastor, heal yourself." In this chapter we wish to examine three approaches he might use to plan some directions for meeting his own needs. First, we will see how he identifies his own pressures, his patterns of coping, and the resources he draws on in his time of need. Second, we will endeavor to identify his idealized and realized priorities and to make those adjustments that are essential to his own personal health and wholeness and his fulfillment in ministry to others. Third, we will examine the role of the laity in his view of the ministry of care.

PRESSURES AND PATTERNS OF COPING

The pastor must take time to introspect and evaluate his own needs and the sources of pressure in his own life. All too often the pastor becomes so overinvolved and overloaded that he takes little time for reflection on his own needs and ways of responding to pressure. As a consequence, he may find himself heavily invested in pastoral responsibilities but carrying around preoccupations, fears, elements of guilt and frustration, which undermine his effectiveness and fulfillment in ministry. The following exercise is intended to assist the pastor in the process of identifying three important factors influencing these concerns:

—the pressures
—patterns of coping
—resources utilized

The following steps are suggested for the effective utilization of the sentence completion test:

Step One

Complete all twelve items as spontaneously as possible, writing each one out on a separate piece of paper. Maintain the number of each item.

Step Two

Write out each item four additional times on the separate sheets of paper. Complete these sentence items reflectively. This will provide you with a total of five responses for each item on the test.

Step Three

Separate these responses into three groups:

Group One—Items 4, 6, 9, 10, 11
Group Two—Items 5, 7, 8, 12
Group Three—Items 1, 2, 3

SENTENCE COMPLETION TEST FOR PASTORS

1. The person I talk with when I am depressed is _____

_____

2. If I were to share my deepest needs, I feel people would think _____

_____

3. I don't want to share with my pastor peers because ____

_____

4. I am preoccupied with _____

5. When I feel down, I _____

6. I feel most guilty about _____

7. I wish there were ways I could _____

_____

8. I invest my greatest degree of emotional energy in ____

_____

9. I worry most about _____

10. That which generally frustrates me the most is _____

_____

11. That which makes me feel like a failure is _____

12. I feel happiest when _____

   The pastor finds it difficult to respond to the above test without mixing his personal and professional experiences. The apostle Paul helps us recognize the presence of the human element in our ministries.

For we preach not ourselves, but Christ Jesus the Lord; and ourselves your servants for Jesus' sake. For God, who commanded the light to shine out of darkness, hath shined in our hearts, to give the light of the knowledge of the glory of God in the face of Jesus Christ. But we have this treasure in earthen vessels, that the excellency of the power may be of God, and not of us. We are troubled on every side, yet not distressed; we are perplexed, but not in despair; persecuted, but not forsaken; cast down, but not destroyed; always bearing about in the body the dying of the Lord Jesus, that the life also of Jesus might be made manifest in our body.[1]

The pressures

The reality is that the pastor does become troubled, perplexed, persecuted, and cast down. Paul is addressing himself to the forces, pressures, and powers that work against him in the proclamation of the gospel. What are pastors preoccupied with? What are the sources of guilt, worry, and frustration in their lives? What brings them to the edge of defeat? It helps a pastor to know that he is not alone in his struggle.

1. *Preoccupations*

Item 4 on the test identifies the pastor's preoccupations. Review your responses to this item, beginning with your spontaneous response and then the four more reflective responses. Compare your preoccupations with some common responses. I am preoccupied with:

—managing all the roles of being a pastor
—my future (I am forty-nine and who will want me or give me a place to serve when I am sixty?)
—my family demands in relationship to church responsibilities
—my self-image and success and how to measure it
—sermon preparations
—the overwhelming needs and demands of my people

2. *Guilt*

Item 6 identifies the guilt factor in life. Review your

responses to this item and compare them with the common concerns of pastors. I feel most guilty about:

—my lack of a consistent devotional life
—the lack of growth in my church
—my anger
—not working constantly
—lustful thoughts or sexual fantasies
—preoccupations with myself
—not disciplining myself better
—my neglect of my wife and children

3. *Worry*

Item 9 on the test focuses the worries of pastors. I worry most about:

—my future in the church
—my family problems
—my church board
—finances
—my wife's emotional and physical condition
—the breakdown of the family in our society
—whether we will be able to keep our doors open

4. *Frustrations*

Item 10 is intended to sharpen our awareness of the sources of frustration in our lives. Review your responses in relationship to those of other pastors.

That which generally frustrates me the most is:

—my inability to communicate with my wife and children
—the church treasurer
—the resistance and unfair criticism by people in the church
—the lack of responsiveness of the congregation
—the double standard of my people
—the unrealistic expectations of the church
—the fact that my marriage is not the model it should be to the congregation

—my own unrealistic expectations of people, particularly of my own family (I can't seem to control it.)

5. *Failure*

Item 11 enables us to identify what it is that makes us feel as though we have failed or are inadequate. Compare your responses to those of other pastors. That which makes me feel like a failure is:

—having peaked at forty-eight
—the low statistics of our church
—when I see so little evidence of people committing themselves to God under my ministry
—when my wife points out my weaknesses in areas of family life
—when the church board doesn't cooperate with my proposals
—when people in the church criticize me
—when I repeat the same mistakes I made in my last parish

These responses put us in touch with the multifaceted pressures and introspections of the clergy.

Patterns of coping

The apostle Paul asserts that while troubled, perplexed, persecuted, and cast down, the servant of God continues to witness to the power of the gospel. He declares that the power of faith is a commitment to a higher order of values and priorities. However, there is that underlying reality that man is the "earthen vessel." What does the pastor do when he feels perplexed and "cast down"? What are his perceptions as to what would help him cope better? What brings him into an experience of relaxation and happiness? Items 5, 7, 8, and 12 are intended to describe by example how pastors see themselves handling their own needs and feelings.

1. *When depressed*

Pastors do get discouraged and many know the power

of depression, even within the life of faith and service. Compare your responses with a sample of pastors. Item 5 identifies that "cast down" condition. When I feel down, I:

- —want to withdraw from people
- —share it with the Lord
- —eat, sleep, and watch TV
- —become quiet and want to get away
- —am full of self-pity
- —tough it out alone
- —play tennis or work my way out of it
- —become irritable and impatient with people
- —have temptations to quit
- —talk it out with someone I can trust

2. Coping

If a pastor were to prescribe ways that would enable him to cope more effectively, what practical changes would he identify with? While suggesting what the medicine should be, he does not always fill the prescription. A sample of pastors responded to item 7 stating, I wish there were ways I could:

- —change the norms for measuring success
- —continue my education so that I might feel more competent
- —experience more success in building up the membership of the church
- —get free of political pressures in the life of the church
- —learn how to better communicate and build personal relationships
- —build stability and cohesiveness into my staff
- —relax
- —accept what is
- —spend more time with my wife and family
- —establish a close friendship with another couple
- —know if other men have gone through what I am experiencing

3. Energy investment

The pattern of energy investment we undertake reveals much about how we handle the outside demands and personal priorities of our lives. It is critical that the pastor evaluate the relationship between his goals and his behavior. Sometimes his energy investment is inconsistent with his personal and professional priorities. Item 8 begins to identify these patterns. I invest the greatest degree of emotional energy in:

—preaching preparation
—one-to-one counseling and calling
—trying to satisfy the people of my church
—helping my wife cope with the kids
—meditating and sorting out directions
—my marital and family needs
—meeting the peripheral demands of the church program
—administration, which demands too much of my time

Even this small sample presents a picture of mixed personal and professional patterns of time and energy investment. This tension between the idealized and realized priorities will be explored more fully in the next section of this chapter.

4. Happiness is

What are the sources of satisfaction, contentment, and fulfillment in the lives of clergy? Perhaps the laity would be surprised by the responses of a sample group of pastors. I feel happiest when:

—I'm catching fish
—a person accepts Christ
—digging in the garden and watching things grow
—I'm out of town, away from the demands of the parish
—I am preaching
—I receive public affirmations, which I need
—I establish and follow an acceptable schedule
—I get away with my family
—alone in the woods

—my relationship with my wife is strong
—close to God and faithful in His service

Resources utilized

As we have followed the journey of the pastor through his personal psychosocial history, we have become increasingly aware of the needs, tasks, and crises confronting him. We have captured the courage and faith of this man as he turns the practical process of life into a spiritual pilgrimage. His need for support and care directly reflects his participation in the human predicament, his commitment to the community of faith. Who will minister to this servant of God and man? When he has touched others until his strength goes out from him, who will touch him? Even Jesus took time to go into the wilderness to rest and gain the strength of a renewed faith and perspective. The Lord Himself passed through the crowd and disappeared from their sight. He had his support group of disciples, although they leaned on Him much of the time. One wonders if there may not have been times when the Lord opened up to His disciples to let them know that He, too, was touched by the same infirmities and pressures.

1. *The significant resource person*

Item 1 on the sentence completion test identifies the person the pastor turns to in his time of need. The person I talk with when I am depressed is:

   —my wife
   —another pastor
   —the ministerial group
   —a pastor in another denomination
   —my dad
   —a counselor

The overwhelming majority of the married clergy identified the wife as the person with whom they shared their deepest problems and frustrations. Many of these pastors expressed some guilt about adding to her emotional overload and contributing to her feelings of separation from the congregation. Another common response is that pastors often feel more comfortable with clergy of other denominations.

2. *Barriers*

One of the immediate questions asked is why the pastor feels inhibited in seeking support and care for himself. Item 2 on the test helps to clarify the nature of these barriers. If I were to share my deepest needs, I feel people would think:

—I am not qualified to meet their needs
—I am weak and self-centered
—less of me
—that I lack a strong faith
—I'm honest and approachable
—I'm incompetent
—I am inconsistent

Another set of responses clarifies why other clergy are not identified more frequently as key resource persons. What are the barriers to the development of the ministry of the brother-priest? Item 3 states that I don't want to share with my pastor peers because:

—they tend to judge and categorize one another
—I fear not being accepted by them afterward
—it may be used against me indirectly in another setting
—they tend to think I am inferior to them
—pastors in my denomination are in bad shape
—they have enough burdens
—they would break the confidence
—I am competitive with them

The sentence completion test has captured some of the pastors' experiences with pressure, his patterns of coping, and his approach to support in meeting his personal needs.

REORDERING THE PRIORITIES

The examination of your personal psychosocial tasks in relationship to the demands and pressures of the ministry often leads to the realization that the priorities of your life have become disordered. The reordering of one's priorities becomes a major ongoing life task. While support and consultation will be important to this process, the initiation of a program for stress reduction rests with the pastor himself. The following five-step program is recommended as the pastor sets out to reorder priorities and reduce stress.

Step 1

Identify your idealized priorities for leading a balanced and fulfilled personal and professional life. List these priorities on the basis of what would meet your personal needs and the demands of the ministry. It is important to note that there are times in a person's life when this is not easy to do. The person who is overloaded and/or depressed generally finds it difficult to gain a perspective on his priorities; and in some cases, supportive counseling and consultation may have to be utilized. It is important that these priorities be expressed in specific behavioral terms, that is, in a language that identifies actual areas for implementation. For example, specific scheduled and structured times for rest, recreation, and family needs and interests may be desired. Therefore, list a specific breakdown of the time and energy to be invested in the various functions of the ministry, and give these items priority from one to ten, adding more if necessary.

1. _____
2. _____
3. _____
4. _____
5. _____
6. _____
7. _____
8. _____
9. _____
10. _____

Step 2

We are now concerned with your realized or actual priorities as evidenced in your personal life and ministry. Do a careful time and energy analysis of what you actually invest yourself in doing. A review of your calendar and appointment book will help to focus these patterns of priority. Go back six months and review each week, writing out a composite picture of what your typical week looked like. Do you see any patterns, and what are the specific areas of activity that dominated your schedule? What were the tasks, demands, activities, needs, concerns, and expectations that dominated your thought and behavior? Identify those specific activities that demand the most of you and into which you invest the greatest amount of time and energy.

1. _____
2. _____
3. _____
4. _____
5. _____
6. _____
7. _____
8. _____
9. _____
10. _____

Step 3

Compare the two lists to identify where they correlate and contradict. Having noted the discrepancies between your idealized and realized priorities, identify those items that either are too high or too low in the order.

1. *Items too high in your actual behavior:*

_____

_____

_____

_____

_____

2. *Items too low in your actual behavior:*

_____

_____

_____

_____

List those factors, lifestyle patterns, habits, or circumstances that are disrupting the realization of your idealized priorities.

_____

_____

_____

_____

You may discover that some of your idealized priorities are stress producing and do not reflect a balanced life.

Step 4

The pastor has the dilemma of maintaining the integrity of his personal and professional priorities in relationship to the demands and expectations of his congregation. The object of this step is to clearly focus a contract for reordering those priorities and a program for self-monitoring. One of the more effective ways of coping with stress is to identify the related behavior patterns and to make clear and concrete contracts for change. If you have done a careful and effective job with the first three steps, you are now ready to focus a contract for change.

1. *Goals*

It is unlikely that you will be able to make a dramatic or immediate change in your priorities, and attempting to do so could discourage you and lead to the resurgence of the disordered priorities that now frustrate you. Take one item from your list of those that are too high and another from your list of those that are too low. State two clear and concrete objectives for the next two weeks that will change the position each holds in your daily and/or weekly schedule.

_____

_____

Then, draft some intermediate goals for the next six weeks that may involve both the increase of some activities and the decrease of others. The purpose of this is to enable you to bring your present behavioral priorities into closer correlation with your idealized priorities.

_____

_____

It is important to maintain the short-term goals while pursuing the intermediate goals. Finally, draft some long-range goals for the next three months that represent what major changes you wish to have realized by that date.

_____

_____

The simple yet basic point of this process is that without clear and concrete objectives it is nearly impossible to change habits or well-established patterns of personal and professional activities.

2. *Scheduling and monitoring*

The goals that have been identified should be transferred into both your appointment book and a desk calendar or chart. This will enable you to do the necessary continuous self-monitoring that is essential to the maintenance of behavior change. These goals have now been objectively identified, scheduled, and given priority, leaving you with the responsibility of monitoring. Remember that the changes you are attempting are usually difficult to realize and maintain, which is why we tend to retain our uncomfortable traps and unfulfilled priorities. It is sometimes easier to fail and to remain diffused than to maintain the necessary effort to change life patterns and priorities.

Daily and weekly times need to be set aside for reviewing the goals you have established. It is important that these times be fixed and written in, and it is helpful if they are tied into a time of private meditation.

The process of self-monitoring may put you in touch with ways in which you tend to sabotage your own priorities. Historically you have blamed it on circumstances or on others, only to discover that you overload yourself with mixed priorities and peripheral considerations. This may represent a combination of low-level motivation and mild depression. It is important to recognize the fact that indecisiveness, difficulty with concentration, loss of motivation, and guilt or remorse are some of the symptoms of depression. This is to suggest that if the process of attempting to reorder one's priorities isn't working and these symptoms are present, the pastor may need to seek further help in this process.

Step 5

Few programs involving behavior change are fulfilled or maintained without the presence and resource of a support person or group. While the pastor is often the key person or the catalyst for the care of others, he is often isolated in his own time of need. Due to the overload in caring for others he may in fact reach a point of feeling physically, emotionally, and motivationally exhausted. To whom does he turn?

1. *Support groups*

Whether through informal or formal structure, there are many group resources available to the pastor that are important to this fifth step of maintaining the contract for stress reduction. While the informal groupings at conferences and retreats are an important resource, there are some potential problems with this. One of the major dangers is that these groupings or dyads could become meetings of like-minded and frustrated men who negatively commiserate, leaving them locked into cynicism compounded by some degree of guilt. It is important that the pastor find an opportunity for understanding that would lead to a renewed sense of direction.

The pastor has much in common with other human service providers, such as social workers. Caring and responding to the needs and demands of others becomes central to one's functions and, to some extent, one's identity. Being in that role makes it difficult to shift to being a receiver or to even admit to that need. This individual may give to the extent that he runs out of the personal resources essential to either maintaining motivation or coping with the related stress. Some pastors see their authority and credibility in terms of both giving and not being needy or dependent themselves. Some pastors develop a style of needing to be in charge or in control, to the extent that they take on more authority than is healthy for either them or the church. The dilemma is that this process places him under the pressure to assume ever enlarging responsibilities.

Ministerial fellowship groups, continuing education experiences, and clinical pastoral education are critically important resources to the pastor's growth in self-awareness and professional development. These settings provide the pastor with the support of those dealing with similar needs, tasks, and stress factors. Clinical pastoral education is consistently identified by pastors as a key resource in their own personal self-awareness and effectiveness in caring for others. Many report that their resistance to these groups had been based on feelings of inferiority and the fear of vulnerability.

2. The mentor

The mentor is one who serves as a model, counselor, or guide; a listener with whom you can test out your ideas, plans, and possibilities, as well as the crises which may be blocking these. Many young men in the ministry have become separated from their mentors. He or she may have been a college or seminary professor, a model pastor, or a key lay person in the church. Upon assuming the role of pastor, many either by circumstance or perspective on their own role lose touch with the mentor. This leaves the pastor without an important resource in these early years of ministry. The concept of the apprenticeship is somewhat related to this, inasmuch as it gives the developing professional a sense of back-up resources. The role of an associate serves this end, provided some of the earlier discussed tensions do not contaminate the relationships between senior pastor and associate. Sometimes a denominational leader fills this role, although most pastors find this too politicized to become an effective resource.

3. Brother-priest

One of the generally untapped, yet powerful, resources is the role of the brother-priest. While there are some parallels with the mentor, there are confessional dynamics that make it unique. The brother-priest is the one to whom a pastor might turn in time of spiritual need. This is the one with whom he is able to establish a confidential sacred trust that enables him to sort out his guilt, anger, and confusion. The brother-priest is the one who demonstrates great integrity in his fulfillment of that function. The power is not his but of God; the communication is confidential before God as a sacred trust. While we tend to view this as distinctively the perspective and privilege of the Roman Catholic clergy, there are significant untapped resources for all men in the ministry. The brother-priest could well be the most important support person in this process of reordering one's priorities and directing oneself away from destructive attitudes and patterns of behavior.

While the brother-priest is often older, this need not be the rule. He is not generally a friend since this tends to confuse the nature and purpose of both relationships. Neither does he have to be a pastor in the same denomination. The barriers to

the brother-priest relationship were discussed earlier as:
- —fear of the violation of confidences
- —self-esteem problems that dictate fear and mistrust
- —an idealized view of ministry, which one feels he has violated
- —projection of personal low self-esteem onto the profession in general
- —fear of vulnerability

The confessional element in this relationship carries with it the power to free the pastor from the bondage of doubt and guilt which block his growth and fulfillment in ministry.

4. *Professional counseling*

This process may have opened up some issues you are either having trouble sorting out or integrating into your life. You may see problems with blocked motivation, periodic or chronic depression, or the inability to effectively reorder stress-producing priorities. You may see your ministry as a pattern of compensation for deep feelings of inadequacy and unresolved self-worth problems. There may be patterns of marital and family neglect that you either don't understand or cannot constructively approach. Your ministry to others may represent a deep need for power and control, which has undermined your effectiveness in ministry or your wholeness personally. The prior question to the issue of intimacy is that of identity. Intimacy, whether defined in sexual and marital terms or in loving and serving people, is the question that cannot be effectively addressed until we have dealt with the question of identity. "Loving one's neighbor as oneself" is important to the clergy, too.

The confrontation with some of these issues may serve to focus the need for securing personal, marital, and/or family counseling. The barriers to pursuing this option are particularly great for the clergy who feel both the threat to their credibility and the fear of vulnerability. The tragedy is that this man who gives and cares so much becomes increasingly locked into his loneliness and stress.

RENEWAL THROUGH LAITY IN MINISTRY

The relationship between the laity and the ordained ministry may become so stratified and/or polarized that it becomes a major source of stress in the pastor's life. The laity tend to place the clergy on a pedestal of such high expectations in areas of behavioral perfection and norms for performance that this becomes a source of pressure for both the pastor and his family. This process becomes translated into a relationship of accountability to the laity, often leading to polarizations of purpose and persons. These forces serve to separate the clergy from the supportive fellowship of the "community" and the laity from the ministries of the church. There are in fact some laymen who see their role as being guardians of the rights and needs of the church, with some degree of mistrust in the pastor's capacity or commitment to those ends. The expectations tend to shift from congregation to congregation, depending on the social and political power base of that particular church. When the clergy become subjected to this kind of pressure, the capacity to creatively minister is undermined.

It may be that the pastor is contributing to the tensions over expectations and responsibilities by stratifying roles and neglecting the delegation of authority and opportunity for ministries. The workaholic-type personality may hold on to authority and responsibilities, leading the laity to feel locked out of the ministry of the church. It is also important for him to determine whether his perceptions of the congregation's expectations are accurate. A pastor who had a disappointing prior parish experience may bring the insecurity and hurt over into the next parish.

It often takes a few years for a pastor and a congregation to establish the rapport, self-awareness, and mutual respect essential to the realization of an effective shared ministry. The goal of this process is the cooperative sharing of their diverse and rich gifts in the fulfillment of the call to the ministries of healing, sustaining, guiding, and reconciling care.[2] Nothing reduces stress in the life of the minister more dramatically than for him to be a part of a community of faith that is actively expressing these functions of the ministry of care. The following questionnaires, on the care ministries of the church, are intended to assist the church in this process of evaluating, focusing, and directing its ministries. They are only tools and need some adaptation to each parish. Each of the sections of the questionnaires has a category identified as *other*, to which more than one item may be added and averaged into the total. This instrument might be used by the minister, the staff, the church board, or the congregation to begin the process of exploring their mutual ministries of care.

QUESTIONNAIRE FOR THE EVALUATION OF CARE MINISTRIES OF THE CHURCH

Answer these questions using the following codes:

0--never in evidence
1--seldom
2--occasionally
3--quite regularly
4--continuously and ongoing

I. HEALING FUNCTIONS OF THE CHURCH (restoring health and wholeness):

Code #

1. Physical healing activities
   a. Encouraging and supporting people to seek necessary medical care   _____
   b. Praying for the healing of the sick without undermining appropriate medical care   _____
   c. Supporting people financially for costs related to the illness   _____
   d. Giving time and providing resources for those who come home to recuperate by

such acts as: home visits, house care, food preparations, child care, spiritual support   ——
  e. Other   ——

Subtotal   ——
Divide by total items
for average   ——

2. Psychological healing activities
   a. Providing prayer support for those struggling with either physical or emotional problems   ——
   b. Supporting the individual in seeking the necessary mental health resources   ——
   c. Sponsoring or supporting a church-related counseling center   ——
   d. Maintaining contact with and support of those hospitalized with mental health problems   ——
   e. Caring and counseling activities are carried on by members of the ministerial staff   ——
   f. Evidence of laity involvement in visitation   ——
   g. Evidence of laity involvement in supportive counseling   ——
   h. Other   ——

Subtotal   ——
Divide by total items
for average   ——

3. Social healing activities
   a. Evidencing a sensitivity to the social needs of the community through prayer   ——
   b. Cooperating with those community organizations that are human service oriented   ——
   c. Providing the social resources and care essential to the individual's adjustments in the community (i.e., home care, child care,

old-age care, transportation to and from
outside resources) _____

d. Providing some contingency fund for
specific needs of the congregation and
community _____

e. Functioning as an advocate group for those
unjustly treated or unrecognized in educational and social services _____

f. Other _____

Subtotal _____

Divide by total items
for average _____

Overall Total for Items 1, 2, 3 _____

Overall Average for Items 1, 2, 3 _____

Relate this average to the code for a sense of the overall healing ministries of the church. Spiritual healing functions will be dealt with under Reconciling Ministries.

II. SUSTAINING FUNCTIONS OF THE CHURCH: (standing by supportively in the face of loss)

1. Visiting and sending cards to the hospitalized _____

2. Maintaining contact with those undergoing
terminal illness _____

3. Visiting and providing listening love to the
shut-ins separated from the church activities _____

4. Small group ministries to individuals
struggling with common problems (i.e., alcohol, weight, chronic illness, etc.) _____

5. Providing emotional and spiritual support
for those undergoing grief experience (individual or group support) _____

6. Accepting and integrating separated and
divorced individuals into the fellowship of
the church _____

7. Providing significant support for children and teens who are feeling the impact of separation and divorce   _____
8. Standing by in both tangible and supportive ways when job loss affects an individual and family   _____
9. Providing all the resources of the church to enable individuals to cope with physical handicaps   _____
10. Other   _____

Total for Section II   _____
Average for Section II   _____

Relate this average to the code for a sense of the overall sustaining ministries of the church.

III. GUIDING FUNCTIONS OF THE CHURCH (providing education, direction, hope, and good models):

1. Providing strong programs for the Christian education of the children and young people of the church   _____
2. Providing teachers who are strong examples of spiritual health and wholeness   _____
3. Providing staff members who work with the junior high and senior high young people, actively coordinating programs, building rapport, and providing guidance and support   _____
4. Utilizing lay workers to provide similar strengths to the young people   _____
5. Avoiding total segregation of the various age groups of the church in order to provide the resources of the older members of the church to those at every age and stage of life   _____
6. Evidence that the young people are given support and guidance in dealing with the power of the media and other institutions in sorting out their values and identity   _____

7. Evidence that the young people are reflecting the principles and values of the church family _____
8. Premarital counseling _____
9. Premarital growth groups through either the local church or cooperating churches _____
10. Sponsoring or cooperating with programs of marital enrichment _____
11. Sponsoring or cooperating with programs for family enrichment _____
12. Developing small group networks throughout the ministries of the church to every age group providing means of increased self-awareness and spiritual maturity _____
13. Other _____

Total for III _____
Average for III _____

Relate this average to the code for a sense of the overall guiding ministries of the church.

IV. RECONCILING FUNCTIONS OF THE CHURCH:

1. A community with strong cohesiveness and few, if any, divisions _____
2. Handles differences with a spirit of openness and forbearance _____
3. Forgiving spirits are evident in how the community handles its problems in relationships _____
4. Individuals or small cliques do not dominate the church _____
5. Confrontational love is expressed through appropriate channels _____
6. Evidences a moral consistency without judgmental or divisive attitudes toward others in the church _____

7. Gifted witnessing laymen who do not create a climate for the devaluation of others who are not so gifted   _____

8. Gifted nurturing laymen who evidence these strengths in building up new Christians in the faith   _____

9. Relating all ministries to the ultimate question of man's reconciliation with God   _____

10. Children are in the church who come from broken families   _____

11. Teens are finding acceptance and support in facing the major problems of home and community   _____

12. Separated and divorced persons are accepted and integrated into the fellowship and programs of the church   _____

13. There are couples in the church whose marriages have been strengthened by the church   _____

14. Commitments to God are continuing to be expressed through renewal services   _____

15. Testimonies to private personal experiences of God's grace are shared to the strengthening of the fellowship of the church   _____

16. Other   _____

Total for IV   _____
Average for IV   _____

Relate this average to the code for a sense of the overall reconciling ministries of the church.

These ministries of healing, sustaining, guiding, and reconciling love represent the power of the gospel to bring wholeness to man's brokenness, comfort and hope where there is despair, purpose where there is confusion, and reunion where there is division and estrangement. The stress of conflicting expectations and demands has too long taken its toll on the ministry. It is time for the laity and the clergy to unite in a shared sense of community and ministry. The tasks and needs confronting the pastor confront his people also, giving them both the potential for empathy and love. There is that strong undergirding of faith and love, enabling and renewing them at each stage of the journey. There is the danger that we lose our vision and become overwhelmed by those forces that divide us. Faith and hope operate even when we lose our way and slip in the pain of the struggle. That hope is based on a sense of a covenant with God, so that at any point in this pilgrimage, whether at the beginning looking ahead with a vision, or at the end looking back with a dream, the God of love and grace is our Alpha and our Omega.

QUESTIONNAIRE FOR EVALUATION OF CARE MINISTRIES OF THE CHURCH

Answer these questions using the following code:

0--never
1--seldom
2--occasionally
3--quite regularly
4--continuously or ongoing

I. HEALING FUNCTIONS OF THE CHURCH (seeking to restore wholeness and health):

(Print in number)

1. Physical healing activities
   a. Encouraging and supporting people to seek necessary medical care _____
   b. Praying for the healing of the sick without cutting them off from medical resources _____
   c. Healing services with an openness to the above _____

d. Supporting people financially for medical costs _____

e. Giving time and providing energy for those who come home to recuperate by such acts as home visits, house care, food preparations, child care, spiritual support _____

f. Other _____

            Subtotal _____

(Divide by total items) Average _____

2. Psychological healing activities

a. Providing spiritual resources for the healing of the person's inner life through prayer and counsel _____

b. Encouraging referral to the necessary mental health resources _____

c. Sponsoring or supporting a church-related counseling center _____

d. Supporting and encouraging those going through hospitalization for emotional difficulties when appropriate _____

e. Visiting those institutionalized whether in a state or private facility when we have cleared with the appropriate people (working through the pastor) _____

f. Caring and counseling activities are carried on my members of the staff _____

g. Other _____

            Subtotal _____

(Divide by total items) Average _____

3. Social healing activities

a. Evidencing a sensitivity to the social needs of the community through prayer _____

b. Evidencing a sensitivity to the social needs of the community by cooperating with

other organizations that are service
oriented   _____

c. Providing transportation, sitting assistance, and home care enabling individuals to function more actively in coping with their situation   _____

d. Channeling some income into social programs to meet the physical, social, and family needs of members of the church and community   _____

e. Participating in communication to leaders to effect change in the plight of members of the community   _____

f. Functioning as an advocate or advocate group for those unjustly treated or unrecognized in services provided   _____

g. Other   _____

Subtotal   _____

(Divide by total items) Average   _____

OVERALL TOTAL FOR 1, 2, 3   _____

(Divide overall total by total items)
OVERALL AVERAGE   _____

Relate the average to the code for a sense of overall giftedness and quality of healing ministries of the congregation.

II. SUSTAINING FUNCTIONS OF THE CHURCH (standing by supportively in the face of loss and its struggle):

1. Visiting and sending cards to the hospitalized undergoing terminal disease process   _____

2. Visiting and communicating appropriately with the elderly who are shut-in and thus separated from a support community   _____

3. Coordinating such activities through a small group that follows through on its ministries   _____

4. Rallying to the emotional and spiritual support of those undergoing a grief experience _____
5. Continuing to provide such support long after the funeral and the departure of family and friends _____
6. Accepting and integrating separated and divorced individuals into the fellowship of the church _____
7. Providing significant support for children and teens who are feeling the impact of separation and divorce in their family _____
8. Standing by in tangible and supportive ways those who have experienced a job loss or disappointment _____
9. Providing all the resources of the church to enable individuals to cope with physical handicaps _____
10. Other _____

Total _____

(Divide by total items in Sec. II) Average _____

Relate average to code for sense of overall giftedness and quality of sustaining ministries of the congregation.

III. GUIDING FUNCTIONS OF THE CHURCH:

1. Providing strong programs for the Christian education of the children _____
2. Providing strong models for teachers who teach us much by healthful spiritual wholeness as by method _____
3. Providing staff members who work with the junior high and senior high young people actively coordinating programs, building rapport, and providing guidance and support _____
4. Utilizing lay leaders to work with the teens who also provide the above strengths _____

5. Avoiding the segregation of church members by age to the extent that the older members are not available examples and advisers   _____

6. The young people are responding to our message and are finding support in dealing with the culture and the media which has such a continuous shaping influence in their lives   _____

7. The young people are reflecting the principles and values of the church family (assuming these to be Christian)   _____

8. Providing guidance resources in the form of support groups for young couples (i.e., premarital growth groups, whether sponsored by the church or interdenominational in make-up)   _____

9. Either sponsoring or cooperating in programs of marital enrichment experience for growth motivated couples in the church   _____

10. Developing small group networks throughout the ministries of the church to every age group providing support and the means of growth in self-awareness and spiritual maturity   _____

11. Other   _____

Total   _____

(Divide by total items)   Average   _____

Relate average to code for sense of overall giftedness and quality of guiding ministries of the congregation.

IV. Reconciling Functions of the Church:

1. Characterized as a church with strong cohesiveness and few if any divisions or tensions   _____

2. Handling differences with a spirit of openness and forbearance   _____

3. Forgiving spirits are evident in how the community handles its problems in relationships _____

4. We do not allow the divisions of individuals or small cliques to dominate the body-life of the church _____

5. Handling such situations with confrontational love through the appropriate channels _____

6. Consistently relating the quality of our relationships with one another to the quality of our relationships with God _____

7. Practicing a religious lifestyle that does not lead to judgmental attitudes and polarizations within the community of faith _____

8. Gifted soul winners are in evidence within our fellowship who do not create a climate for devaluation of others who are not so gifted. _____

9. Gifted nurturing Christians who evidence their strengths in building and nurturing new Christians in the faith _____

10. Relating all of our ministries to the ultimate question of man's reconciliation with God _____

11. Those ministered to (i.e., in the other dimensions of care) naturally move toward the fellowship of the church _____

12. There are children in our church who come from divided families _____

13. There are teens who are finding acceptance and support in the face of major problems in home and community _____

14. Separated and divorced people are accepted and evidence positive faith response in discipleship and commitment _____

15. There are couples in our church who would not likely be together were it not for the ministries of the church _____

16. Commitments to God are continuing to be expressed through healthy revival and renewal services   _____

17. Testimonies as to private personal encounters with God are continuing to be shared   _____

18. Other   _____

Total   _____

(Divide by total items)   Average   _____

Relate average to code for sense of overall giftedness and quality of reconciling ministries of the congregation.

SENTENCE COMPLETION TEST FOR PASTORS

Complete the following statements as spontaneously as possible.

1. The person I talk with when I am depressed or discouraged is _____

2. If I were to share my deepest needs, I feel people would think _____

3. I don't want to share with my pastor peers because _____

4. I am preoccupied with _____

5. When I feel down, I _____

6. I feel most guilty about _____

7. I wish there were ways I could _____

8. I invest my greatest degree of emotional energy in _____

9. I worry most about _____

10. That which generally frustrates me the most is _____

_____

11. That which makes me feel like a failure is _____

_____

12. I feel happiest when _____

_____

Notes

Chapter 1

[1]Jeremiah 8:18 (KJV).
[2]Jeremiah 9:2 (KJV).
[3]Luke 4:18-19 (LIVING BIBLE).
[4]Luke 4:23-24 (LIVING BIBLE).
[5]Luke 4:30.
[6]Jeremiah 9:2 (KJV).
[7]Acts 13:51.
[8]Friedman, M. and Rosenman, R.H. *Type A Behavior and Your Heart.* New York: Knopf, 1974. Selye, Hans. *The Stress of Life* (rev. ed.). New York: McGraw-Hill, 1978.
[9]Tillich, Paul. *The New Being.* New York: Charles Scribner's Sons, 1955, p. 41.

Chapter 2

[1]Proverbs 29:18 (KJV).
[2]Amos 8:11 (KJV).
[3]Erikson, Erik H. *Childhood and Society* (2nd. ed.). New York: W.W. Norton, 1964, p. 263.
[4]Ibid., pp. 247-263.
[5]Ibid.
[6]Mark 9:24 (KJV).
[7]Erikson, Erik H. *Insight and Responsibility.* New York: W.W. Norton, 1964, p. 128.
[8]Havighurst, R.J. *Developmental Tasks and Education* (3rd. ed.). New York: McKay, 1972.
[9]Levinson, D.J., et al. *The Seasons of a Man's Life.* New York: Knopf, 1978, pp. 90f.
[10]Ibid.
[11]Havighurst, *Developmental Tasks and Education.*
[12]Erikson, *Insight and Responsibility,* p. 128.
[13]Ibid.
[14]Levinson, et al. *The Seasons of a Man's Life.* Sheehy, Gail. *Passages.* New York: E.P. Dutton, Bantam Edition, 1977.
[15]Levinson, *Seasons of a Man's Life,* p. 90.
[16]Joel 2:28-32.
[17]Keniston, K. *Youth and Dissent: The Rise of a New Opposition.* New York: Harcourt, Brace, Jovanovich, 1971.
[18]John 17.
[19]Keniston, K. *The Uncommitted: Alienated Youth in American Society.* New York: Dell, 1967.

[20]Rogers, Carl R. *On Becoming a Person: A Therapist's View of Psychotherapy*. Boston: Houghton Mifflin, 1961, p. 185.
[21]Rogers, Carl R. *Client-Centered Therapy*. New York: Houghton Mifflin, 1951, p. 151.
[22]Ibid., p. 437.

Chapter 3

[1]Levinson, *Seasons of a Man's Life*, p. 222.
[2]Erikson, *Childhood and Society*, pp. 266-268.
[3]Thoreau, Henry David. *Walden and Civil Disobedience*. New York: New American Library, 1960, p. 10.
[4]Ibid.
[5]Levinson, *Seasons of a Man's Life*, p. 209.
[6]Ibid., p. 210.
[7]Mayer, Nancy. *The Male Mid-Life Crisis*. New York: Doubleday and Company, 1978, p. 189.
[8]Friedman and Rosenman, *Type A Behavior and Your Heart*.
[9]Erikson, *Childhood and Society*, p. 267.
[10]Havighurst, *Developmental Tasks and Education*.
[11]Levinson, *Seasons of a Man's Life*, pp. 228f.
[12]Ibid., p. 239.

Chapter 4

[1]Atchley, Robert C. *The Social Forces in Later Life* (2nd. ed.). Belmont: Wadsworth Publishing Co., 1977, p. 210.
[2]Ibid., p. 209.
[3]Ibid., p. 212.
[4]Ibid.
[5]1 Corinthians 13:7-8a (Phillips).

Chapter 5

[1]2 Corinthians 4:5-10 (KJV).
[2]Clebsch, W.A. and Jaekle, C.R. *Pastoral Care in Historical Perspective*. Englewood Cliffs: Prentice-Hall, 1964, pp. 33-66.